JARGONBUSTING
THE ANALYST'S GUIDE TO
TEST CRICKET

JARGONBUSTING
THE ANALYST'S GUIDE TO
TEST CRICKET
SIMON HUGHES

First published in 2001 by Channel 4 Books, an imprint of Macmillan Publishers Ltd, 25 Eccleston Place, London SW1W 9NF, Basingstoke and Oxford.

Associated companies throughout the world.

www.macmillan.com

ISBN 0 7522 1946 4

Text © Simon Hughes, 2001

9 7 5 3 1 2 4 6 8

A CIP catalogue record for this book is available from the British Library.

Design by

studio **cactus** Ⓒ

Stills © The England & Wales Cricket Board courtesy of Channel 4, BBC and TWI except those listed on page 160.
Printed and bound in Great Britain by Bath Press

CONTENTS

Foreword

by Mark Nicholas

Last May at the Grosvenor House Hotel in London, the words ' ... and the BAFTA for Best Sports Programme goes to – Channel 4 Cricket' ripped an electric shock through a table of bright, dedicated people whose work and dreams had been acknowledged at the highest seat.

It was an extraordinarily gratifying moment and, I believe, a significant statement for the game in general. Over fifteen years or so cricket had drifted away from the people. Increasingly seen as expensive and elitist, assumed to be the property of public schools and private clubs, the state was all but ignoring it. Talk of the game was dark or, worse, uninterested. The failures of the national team were humiliating.

From a late October morning in 1998 when I began my own relationship with Channel 4, the idea was to make the coverage of cricket livelier and more approachable, to demystify but not patronise, to sparkle and sell without hype or trickery. Yes, there would be technology, gimmicks if you like – red zones, snickometers and speedos – but only to enhance the images and words, not to usurp them. Alongside the snickometer moments there was the Saturday morning Roadshow, the Analyst, Jargonbusting, a sympathetic interview, an original feature, an e-mail question answered.

We were determined that cricket should not be stuffy; that children who watched once would choose to watch again; that women, who traditionally make up only a small percentage of the audience, would want to know more. The Roadshow, with its fast-increasing viewing figures, appears to provide the lighter yet still informative feel that has encouraged a wider audience. Another revealing aspect was that much of the early euphoria over the coverage came from the players themselves who trusted the screen and happily began to sell its message themselves.

The knock-on effects continue, recently Channel 4 joined with the English Cricket Board and Lambeth City Council in researching and, hopefully, providing a cricket facility to satisfy the massive desire for the game in inner-city areas such as Brixton in south London where The Oval is the only cricket ground.

It may only be the beginning. Technology is bringing in exciting changes in the way we watch sport. Choice, interaction and access are all embryonic. 3D images cannot be a mile away and fascinating additions such as Hawkeye for lbws in cricket and Accu Call in tennis are around the corner.

What's more you'll get it all on the Internet soon, clear as a bell. And won't that be a thing, settling on an aeroplane, foraging through the bush or drifting across an ocean (if only!) to the sight and sound of Darren Gough blitzing out Steve Waugh's middle-stump. And this book, of course, should help you to understand just how he does it.

Introduction

'Classic swing! It reversed into him and bowled him leg stump through the gate...'

Cricket is full of mysterious skills and baffling terms that sometimes make watching it a turn off. This book is an aid to understanding what's going on out there. It's not a text book or a coaching manual, full of static theories and techniques and advice about how to play the cover drive. It's not about rights and wrongs. It explores individuality and the nuances of Test cricket, using actual televised examples taken from recent England matches both at home and abroad. It attempts to demystify the complex methods and terminology that make cricket such an inaccessible game.

A Test match day contains over 500 deliveries, yet one piece of action takes less than five seconds. This book lingers over those fleeting moments, looking at a complex game from every conceivable angle, trying to convey the real art of cricket. A massive amount of thought and expertise is crammed into each delivery and shot. Some are the result of months, maybe years of practice and planning. Ultimately, the game is about a bowler attempting to force a batsman into making a fatal mistake. The strategies and skills he uses to do that, and the batsman's responses, are the essences of Test cricket.

And it's good to report that Test cricket is on the up. At the time of writing, England have signed big new contracts with npower and Vodafone, and the first three days of all the 2001 Ashes Tests are sold out. What's more, after years of procrastination, a world league of Test nations has finally been drawn up, to give the myriad series between the ten countries a focal point and at last redress the imbalance between five-day cricket and one-day cricket.

World Test League by Series (February 2001)

	Played	Won	Drawn	Lost	Points	Average
1. Australia	15	12	1	2	25	1.67
2. South Africa	15	10	2	3	22	1.47
3. West Indies	14	6	3	5	15	1.071
4. Sri lanka	15	6	4	5	16	1.067
5. Pakistan	15	6	2	7	14	0.933
6. England	14	6	1	7	13	0.929
7. New Zealand	16	5	2	9	12	0.75
8. India	15	4	3	8	11	0.73
9. Zimbabwe	14	2	2	10	6	0.43
10. Bangladash	1	0	0	1	0	0.00

The points are awarded two for a series win and one for a draw. It confirms that Australia has been the outstanding team of the last decade and that South Africa are not that far behind. It will take a marked improvement by the rest to knock these two off the top. England might be a little relieved this league table wasn't introduced a year or so ago, when they would have collected the wooden spoon. As it is, early 2001 finds England's cricket on the up.

Increasingly, the world of cricket is a melting pot of skills, and more and more sophisticated planning and preparation. There is a risk, therefore, that those not initiated into the cricketing fraternity will miss out on the drama and diversity of an intriguing game that is as much an examination of character as it is of craft.

Test cricket can seem an alien world where people do odd things and speak a strange language. This is a guidebook to that world, translating useful phrases, showing you the best nooks and crannies, encouraging you to peer under the surface more. I hope you enjoy your visit ...

RAW MATERIALS

Test cricket is a long game, the longest team game competitively played, and you won't necessarily get a winner. It may go to the last ball of the fifth day or it may all be over in two days. It's long but it's also complex, that's what makes it so fascinating. Before moving on to techniques and skills, it helps to have an understanding of some of the basic elements of the game – the pitch, the bat and ball, and some of the most important laws.

The Basics

So many things affect a game of cricket but, apart from the weather, which no one has any control over, the pitch is the biggest variable. No two pitches are the same and no one pitch is the same from one day to the next. The type of pitch (and perhaps the weather forecast) will influence the make-up of a team. As far as the actual bat and ball are concerned, they are much more under the control of the individual player – the ball can be manipulated up to a point, and every batsmen will have his favourite bat, which will be constantly repaired.

The teams

It is only after extensively studying the pitch that the captain can decide on the balance of his team. He must declare it at the toss, half an hour before the start. Five batsmen and a wicket-keeper are taken as read; the main debate is whether to play five bowlers, or four and an extra batsman. It helps if you have a couple of all-rounders, then you can easily get away with four bowlers. These will probably be made up of three main fast bowlers and a spinner, or if the pitch is very green or damp looking, a fourth 'quickie'. Rarely these days do Test teams field five specialist bowlers. During Australia's recent dominance they have consistently relied on three pacemen and a leg spinner.

Batting-wise, you obviously need two specialist opening batsmen, capable of taking the sting out of an attack. Number three is a pivotal position, since he needs to be able to bat like an opener if there's an early wicket, or be more cavalier if he comes in at 140-1. The number four spot is frequently preferred by the best batsman in the side. Here, he's hidden from the vagaries of the new ball, but not too far down the order that he's liable to run out of partners. A sprinkling of left-handed batsmen is always useful.

COMING TOGETHER
This is what the preparation is all about. One team pitting itself against another. The vagaries of the pitch and the weather have been taken into consideration in choosing the teams and now they just have to go out there and win.

The Pitch

'Pitches are like wives, you can never quite tell how they will turn out,' said Sir Len Hutton after asking Australia to bat first in Brisbane and seeing them score 600. The only thing you can be certain about is that they are 22 yards long (between wicket and wicket). Otherwise, each pitch has its own idiosyncrasies, influenced by prevailing weather, soil, groundsman and quiet guidance from the home side. For instance, if the hosts are 2-1 up going into the final Test of a series, it'll be no surprise to find a soft pitch that absolutely guarantees a draw.

There are a variety of pitch-types in England as these four examples of Test pitches from the summer of 2000 show. In early summer, they will be green and dampish but by August they will be dry and brown.

LORD'S
Here, the grass is usually closely cropped and even, but the grey-marl colour suggests dampness underneath.

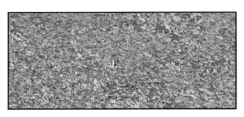

THE OVAL
Here, the grass is patchier and coarser, offering a slow, spongy bounce. It used to be faster but has lost some of its pace.

HEADINGLEY
The surface here is more like crazy paving, with hairline cracks that widen as the game develops.

OLD TRAFFORD
Here, the cracks are quite wide and the ball will misbehave – keeping low or lifting if it lands on the edge.

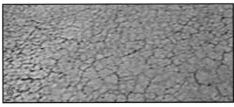

KARACHI
A pitch in Pakistan, just for comparison. The soil is baked solid but the surface, despite its appearance, plays well.

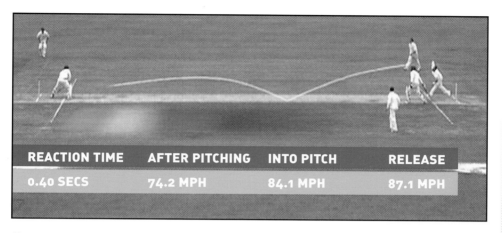

REACTION TIME	AFTER PITCHING	INTO PITCH	RELEASE
0.40 SECS	74.2 MPH	84.1 MPH	87.1 MPH

PACEY PITCH
Old Trafford is quite a pacey surface, this ball from Craig White decelerated by only 10mph after pitching.

Preparing a Test pitch

A Test pitch is played on only once a season in England (harder, longer lasting surfaces in hotter places, like Australia or South Africa, can be used much more often). In England, the groundsman will seed it as soon as possible after it's been used, then nurture it for about eight months through the winter. The following April, rolling will start and continue periodically while the pitch is watered and manicured and left open to the elements. Around ten days before the Test, the watering will stop and the rolling will become more intensive, right up to the morning of the match. It gets its final trim half an hour before play, and is then rolled for seven minutes every morning and before each innings. The captain of the side about to bat can choose what size of roller to use. The arrival at the wicket of a hopeless number 11 batsmen often coincides with the groundsman starting up the roller.

In England, groundsmen make every effort to prepare a dry pitch, but the weather usually conspires against them, and there will generally be a bit of dampness under the surface. This is why the toss is often important. Moisture generally equals movement, and there are various things for the captain to weigh up. Will batting be harder at the beginning when the pitch is fresh and the ball is darting about, or when it's worn and cracked and the ball is bouncing unpredictably? Will the dampness dry out quickly? Will the top surface last? Sometimes it is better to lose the toss and watch the opposition wrestle with the problem.

What all players crave is a bit of pace in a pitch and consistent bounce. No one minds a bit of early dampness or the ball spinning off dusty areas later on. But if it's too slow it's no good for anyone, and if it's cracked or rutted batsmen will be ducking short balls that don't get up and smash into their ribs, or playing forward to ones that lift and jam their fingers against the bat handle. The last thing anyone wants is for the physio to make more appearances than *The Mousetrap*.

Bats and Balls

The bat has had several stages of evolution from the mid-1700s when cricket first became popular and batsmen wielded a curved piece of wood that looked more like a scythe. By the nineteenth century it had taken on a more familiar, if rather flimsy, look, which stayed fairly constant for 100 years.

Bats

It was only in the 1970s – when bowling became faster, batsmen stronger and marketeers more inventive – that significant changes occurred. Bats got thicker and heavier and there were a few gimmicks. The 'scoop', pioneered by Gray Nicholls, had part of its back carved out to improve balance and widen the sweet spot, and Bob Willis, the one-time England captain, emerged with a Duncan Fearnley bat that, to aid balance, was peppered with little holes as if it had been left on a rifle range. Dennis Lillee tried to get away with using an aluminium bat. In the eighties, some batsmen emerged with unwieldy pieces of wood weighing more than 3lb, one-and-a-half times the weight of pre-war bats.

Dimensions

There is actually no restriction on the weight of a bat, the only guidelines relate to size. It must not be more than 38in in length – including the handle – and not more than $4^{1}/_{4}$ in in width. It must also be made of wood (invariably willow). Generally now, players have gone back to lighter bats – around 2lb 6oz, which they find, with modern manufacturing methods, gives them a good balance between 'feel' and power.

The 'sweet spot'

The 'middle' of the bat or 'sweet spot' is its thickest point, usually about 6in from the bottom. Test batsmen are very particular about their own bats and will have bits shaved off the back until they pick up absolutely right. They may also request a higher middle if they are going to be playing in somewhere like Australia where the bounce of the ball is a bit steeper. Although they may have five or six bats on the go at any one time, there will always be a particular favourite, which they will take special care of and have endlessly repaired.

THE MODERN BAT
A modern bat will weigh around 2lb 6oz and be tailored to individual players' preferences.

WEAR AND TEAR
A new ball (right) can be claimed by the fielding side after 80 overs with the old one. The one on the left is probably about 50-overs old. The dryness of the pitch and outfield determines how quickly the ball deteriorates.

The ball

It's red, it's round, it bounces on the ground. It weighs 5½ oz, and is made of leather with a cork core and a flax seam. In Test cricket you can get a new one every 80 overs, although if the spinners are taking wickets, the captain might delay taking it for a while. As you might expect, there's quite a difference between a new ball and one that has been whacked relentlessly into the ground (and into the advertising hoardings). However much you polish an old ball, you aren't going to get much shine.

There are various different makes of ball used in Test cricket. Dukes, which keep their shine longer, are preferred in England. Kookaburra's, which have a prouder seam, are used in Australia. Indian-made balls are more common on the sub-continent because they are harder wearing –

they feel like a lump of concrete hitting the bat. The umpires will present a box of new balls to the fielding side before play, so they can choose the one they want to use. Usually, an opening bowler will select one with a darker hue as it is commonly believed these swing more.

Occasionally, a ball will come apart or go out of shape during play and can be exchanged for one of a similar age. Claiming that the ball is out of shape is sometimes a ruse to get the ball changed because it is flying plumbline straight onto the middle of the bat, and a different one might help the bowlers more. But the umpires generally see through this request and rebuff it. It is perfectly legal to rub sweat or saliva into the ball to polish it. Anything else (sun cream, Vaseline, etc) is forbidden (see Ball Tampering p.92).

The Creases and the Stumps

Two things remain constant in any game of cricket – the markings of the crease and the positioning and dimensions of the stumps. They are both central to the action. The purpose of the crease lines has changed a bit over the years but they have always been there in some form. The stumps are, of course, synonymous with the wicket, they are what the batsman is trying to protect from the bowler.

The creases

These are the white lines you can see around the wicket – there are in fact three creases and they all serve slightly different purposes. The bowling crease is the line that the stumps are on. The line itself is 8ft 8in and the stumps will be in the middle. The popping crease is the line 4ft in front of the bowling crease and the space between the two marks out the batsman's 'ground', the line will be at least 6ft long but is actually considered to be unlimited. The bowler, when he delivers, must not overstep this line (part of his foot must be behind it). It also marks the line the batsman has to cross, with bat grounded, when scoring a run. The return crease is marked at right angles to the other creases, stretching back from the popping crease behind the bowling crease, it forms a line which the bowler's back foot must not cut during delivery.

The stumps

There are three stumps – leg, middle and off – which is which depends on whether the batsman is left- or right-handed. The stumps have to conform to exact specifications. Each stump must be 28in from ground to top. The full width of all three stumps is 9in, evenly spaced, and the two bails sit in grooves on top of the stumps. In order for a batsman to be out bowled, stumped, run out, or hit wicket, at least one bail must be dislodged.

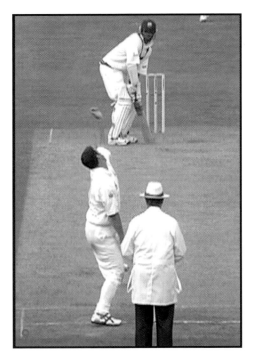

CENTRE OF ATTENTION
The stumps and the creases are crucial to every ball bowled in a match. They are the main focus of the umpire's attention.

Eleven Ways of Being Out

Technically, a batsman isn't out unless there's an appeal to the umpire. In the case of a batsman being clean bowled or some equally obvious dismissal, an appeal isn't necessary.

The Five Most Common Ways of Being Out:

1. Bowled – includes 'played on' when the ball goes from bat onto stumps. A bail must be dislodged.

2. Caught – you can be out caught off the bat or the hand/glove holding the bat.

3. Leg Before Wicket – the ball hitting the leg in front of the stumps (see lbw p.18).

4. Stumped – batsman straying out of his crease when the bails are removed.

5. Run out – batsman attempting to take a run, short of his ground when the wicket is broken.

Four Less Likely:

6. Hit wicket – bat or pads disturbing the stumps and bails falling off. Includes treading on stumps, sometimes the result of fast bowling.

7. Handled the ball – a ball trickling back onto the stumps mustn't be intercepted by hand, only by bat or foot.

8. Hit the ball twice – attempting to gain an unfair advantage by hitting the ball again.

9. Obstructing the field – e.g., stopping a throw reaching the wicket-keeper, with bat or body, or preventing a fielder from taking a catch.

Two Remote Possibilities:

10. Timed out – officially, if a new batsman hasn't arrived in the middle within three minutes of the last wicket, the fielding side can appeal, but on the rare occasion that it has happened in Test cricket, they never have done.

11. Retired out – a batsman can declare his innings over if he's exhausted or wants to give other players a chance. However, this only really happens in warm-up games and is unlikely in Test cricket.

The Lbw Law

Leg before wicket is the most complex law in cricket. Few people really understand it properly, including an alarming number of players and (non-first class) umpires. The first thing an lbw decision needs is an appeal, as in 'Howzatt?', usually from the bowler. Without that, the umpire can't give the batsman out. There have been isolated occasions when an umpire has thought to himself, 'Mmm, that was close, why didn't they appeal?' but it doesn't happen very often.

For an 'out' decision the ball must satisfy certain criteria.

1. It must, in the opinion of the umpire, be going to hit the wicket.

2. It must, if the batsman is playing a shot, have hit him in an imaginary line between wicket and wicket. (If he wasn't playing a shot, he can be out even if it hit him outside this line.)

3. It must not have pitched outside-leg stump.

4. It must not have made contact with the bat before it hit the pad.

If the umpire is unsure about any of these factors, he must give the batsman the benefit of the doubt, which is largely why bowlers always perceive themselves as second-class citizens. Bear in mind that the umpire has a couple of seconds and no replays to make these hairline decisions.

OUT:
This ball pitched outside the off-stump, Michael Vaughan played a shot, it hit his pad in line with the wicket and the umpire decided it would have hit.

NOT OUT:
Although this ball might have hit the wicket, it struck Alec Stewart's pad just outside the line of the stumps. He was playing a shot, so it couldn't be out.

OUT:
Here, contact is again outside the stumps, but Vaughan wasn't offering a shot and if the ball was going to hit the wicket it could be given out.

NOT OUT:
Jimmy Adams, bowling left arm over the wicket, was pitching the ball outside the leg stump from where you can't, in any circumstances, be given out lbw. Stewart was quite safe using his pad

NOT OUT:
The pitching outside leg stump factor is particularly relevant to left handers. Thorpe was lucky, this one pitched a fraction outside leg stump. Therefore, although he would have been bowled, it couldn't be given out.

OUT:
This inswinger (to a left-hander) from Darren Gough satisfied all the requirements. The umpire had his finger up almost as soon as Gough had opened his mouth.

OPENING THE
BATTING

Opening batsmen are quite solitary individuals – you need to have plenty of self-assurance, quite a bit of courage and great powers of concentration. Opening the innings is a huge responsibility. By batting through the first session and blunting the threat of the new ball, they can build a solid platform on which they, and later batsmen, can flourish.

  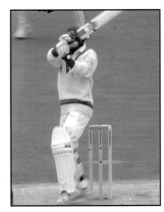

Opening Partnership

Although they will be individualists, opening the batting is a partnership – there are two batsmen and it helps for them to have complimentary styles. A right-handed and left-handed opening pair causes maximum disruption to the bowlers, making it hard for them to establish a rhythm. A solid defensive player, partnering a run-scorer, means the scoreboard keeps ticking over and the bowlers have to alter their tactics for each batsman. Opening batsmen may not be the most prolific run-makers but part of their job is to protect the run-makers in the middle order from the new ball.

Taking guard

The first thing any batsman does when he arrives at the wicket is take his guard. He will hold his bat up vertically and ask the umpire what stump it is covering. He will then scratch or chip a mark on the crease so he knows where to stand and rest his bat in relation to the wicket. Sometimes, if the ground is really hard, he'll hammer a bail in to create a small indent. Batsmen do this so they know the exact whereabouts of the wicket without having to look back all the time. There are a variety of guards; 'two' (bat covering middle and leg stumps) and 'middle' are the most popular.

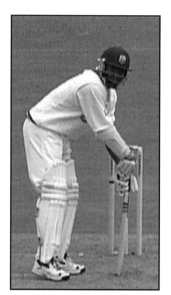

USUAL GUARD
Guard is a habitual thing – most batsmen will fix on their preferred guard early in their career and then stick with it.

MAKING YOUR MARK
During a Test match the crease area soon becomes a mass of overlapping dents and scratches.

Surveying the Field

It's the first over of the innings, and unless he's playing against Bangladesh or Sri Lanka who are not blessed with quick bowlers, a Test opening batsman is bound to be faced with a very attacking field. That means lots of fielders up-close. He'll have a quick glance round to check where they all are.

There will usually be a number of slip catchers (a) and a gully (b), waiting to pouch an edge, as the bowler should get awkward extra bounce and movement with a hard, new ball. A short-leg (c) will usually be deployed to catch anything that balloons off the glove or inside edge, and, in this day and age, give plenty of choice advice to the batsman from under his helmet! With his huge walrus moustache, the Australian David Boon managed to do this without apparently moving his lips. In this example (3), Curtly

Ambrose is bowling to Michael Atherton and a silly point (d) has been brought in, partly to stop Atherton from plunging his front leg forward (and thereby possibly popping up a bat-pad catch), and partly as a distraction to get in his eyeline. The only out-fielders here are cover (e) to stop singles and cut off anything more aggressive, square leg and fine leg (f and g). Although it is quite a threatening field to be faced with, it's a hard one to bowl to because there are so many gaps. The bowler has to be extremely accurate.

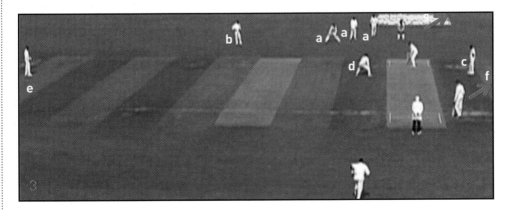

ATTACKING FIELD
This is an attacking field for a new-ball bowler (here Curtly Ambrose). Three slips (a) and a gully (b) is the norm allied to a short leg (c). The silly point (d) is an extra threat, directly in the batsman's eyeline.

KEY			
a	slip catchers	**e**	cover
b	gully	**f**	square leg
c	short leg	**g**	fine leg
d	silly point		

Ultra-attacking

Field settings can get even more aggressive, and when the West Indies at Headingley found themselves 3-2, with Darren Gough on a hat trick this field set for Brian Lara was ultra-attacking (4). A bowler is liable to subconsciously add about 5mph to his pace in this situation. Notice the leg slip here (circled) positioned

because Gough was getting a bit of in-swing to the left-hander. The slips are still there of course, for the ball angled across him, which left-handers are always vulnerable to, and a sort of fifth slip for Lara's angled bat shot. There are either going to be more wickets with a field like this, or the other possibility is lots of runs through all the gaps.

ULTRA-ATTACKING FIELD
England here are all fired up, Gough's on a hat trick and the West Indies are 3-2. They want to keep the pressure on. The leg slip (circled) is a rare position these days, employed here to catch a flick off the toes. In his prolific career, Brian Lara will rarely have encountered a field setting as aggressive as this.

UMBRELLA FIELD
Occasionally in a Test, the batsman doesn't have to look round the field because all the fielders will be in a line, as shown here. This is known as an 'umbrella field' and is only set if the batsman's a renowned mouse, the bowler an absolute demon with a vicious late outswinger (see arrow) and there are runs to play with. It is not a field that an opening batsman would normally face.

Getting Ready – Stance and Backlift

Lindwell

eyes level

head forward

'How d'you play fast bowling?' the great Len Hutton was once asked. 'From the other end,' he replied. Opening batsmen have to face a continuous onslaught of aggressive fast bowling, balls will be bowled at them at speeds of over 90mph – giving them less than 0.4sec to react – and at different heights and angles. To deal with the bowling, the batsman needs to be settled and balanced and have a mental plan for how to cope with whatever's thrown at him.

Upright stance

The modern stance against really fast bowling is an upright position at the crease – eyes level (6) – bat tapping away behind the feet. This is more a nervous habit than any prelude to playing a shot. Michael Atherton looks poised and ready, which you need to be to face a large West Indian about to propel a 85mph missile. He's also standing with his back foot just on the crease line. This is to allow him space to take a reasonable step back if the ball is short, and still be in no danger of treading on the stumps (7, left).

Just before the pace bowler releases, batsmen tend to make a small backward movement (7, centre). Like many others, this is Atherton's way

POISED
Michael Atherton makes a small backward step before the bowler releases, but his weight is still forward.

of giving himself a fraction more time and also to be ready to counter the extra bounce of the new ball (7, right). The key thing about Atherton's position is balance. Although he has stepped back slightly his head is still forward so he can advance towards the ball quickly, if necessary.

Quick feet

Brian Lara takes an even bigger step back but, being unusually nimble and sharp, he can afford to (8). He has a huge, exaggerated backlift – almost like a baseball player's. It enables him to hit the ball hard, but such large, jerky movements also sometimes get him into trouble.

> 'The key to a successful stance is balance and comfort'

READY TO STRIKE
Brian Lara's backlift has more in common with Mark McGuire, baseball's home-run specialist, than cricket. He's been captured here at the top of his dramatic back lift. You know if he lets fly from this position, the ball is going to take some stopping. Early in his innings he takes a backward step and crouches slightly, but later he relaxes and his stance becomes more upright.

How Stance has Changed

It is quite interesting to see how a batsman's initial set-up has changed over time. Though the basics look the same, there are subtle differences in body and bat position, influenced by the type of bowling and fashions of the time. When fast bowling began to dominate in the 1970s, a lot of batsmen made large early movements, with the bat held aloft in readiness for a searing delivery.

W.G. GRACE
The legendary W.G. Grace looks rather hunched and ungainly. However, this loose, crouched stance didn't prevent him making many centuries.

The Australian Don Bradman, who finished his Test career in 1948 with an average of 99.94 runs per innings, stood astride the crease with his bat resting between his legs. Otherwise it was a conventional stance and remained the norm throughout the game until the 1970s (10). Note the lack of helmet or much padding.

The 6ft 6in Tony Greig was the player who broke the mould and opted for a more confrontational approach, bat brandished aloft as the bowler (in this case Dennis Lillee) was about to deliver. This was also partly due to his height. To rest the bat on the ground he had to stoop. This was the start of the dominance of pace.

DON BRADMAN
The undisputed master. Note his small stature, bat resting between his legs, and turned to face mid-wicket.

TONY GREIG
The first player to stand up, bat waving in mid-air before a fast bowler released. It enabled him to be more aggressive.

Graham Gooch began his career standing in the traditional way, slightly bent over the bat on the ground (12), during his Test debut against Australia. However, as he was out twice for nought in that game, it was perhaps not surprising that he soon adopted Greig's more upright method. And, with the aid of a heavy bat and a lot of courage, Gooch was one of the only men to put the terrifying West Indies pace attacks of the 1980s to the sword (13).

Peter Willey (now a Test umpire) was another courageous batsman, prepared to take on any pace attack. He evolved a weird stance that involved standing with his chest and knees pointing down the wicket and shoulders angled towards mid-wicket. He found this position made it easier to get his hands and bat 'high' when a fast ball lifted towards his chest (14).

GRAHAM GOOCH
In the 1970s Gooch was stooped and static (12). In the 1980s he got his 3lb bat up early and became prolific (13).

PETER WILLEY
A brave cricketer, Willey developed this strange 'front-on' method to enable him to stand up to fast bowling. He could get the bat virtually above his head to fend off lifting deliveries.

Defence

In England's recently completed three Test series in Pakistan, there were over 5,000 'dot' balls (balls not scored off, recorded by a dot in the scorebook). This is the equivalent of 10 days cricket without a run. It sounds tedious, and obviously would be if they were all back to back, but it illustrates the importance of building a Test innings brick by brick. Without a sound defence, you can't do this. Test-class bowling is too good to allow a shot a ball. Even the most fluent scoring batsmen – men like Viv Richards and Brian Lara – need to be able to block the best deliveries.

Leaving the ball

In the first few overs of a Test, an opening batsman would prefer to leave as many balls as possible alone. (The bowler, of course, will try to make him play). This allows him to gauge the behaviour of the pitch, the pace of the bowlers and what sorts of shots are going to be safe. There are many ways of leaving the ball.

Shouldering arms

The most common evasive action is 'shouldering arms' – literally raising the bat to shoulder level to let the ball pass by (15). The bat is already raised at waist level, or higher, in the backlift, and if the ball is so wide it doesn't demand a shot, the batsman just leaves his bat where it is, rather than bringing it down. It's dangerous to make this decision too early in the ball's flight, though. Twice in one Test Mike Gatting was deceived by Malcolm Marshall's late inswing and, shouldering arms, was lbw offering no shot. There are other ways of avoiding the ball – some more digni-fied than others (to duck is a natural instinct, but not without its dangers).

UNDERNEATH
Shouldering arms to a ball just wide of the stumps (15) requires good judgement.

OVER THE TOP
Early in an innings most batsmen will look to avoid bouncers by getting underneath them (16). Leaving your bat up can be dangerous though.

TO PLAY OR NOT TO PLAY
Marcus Trescothick (17) shows a precious ability not to flirt with good balls outside off-stump. Nick Knight (18), however, seems sometimes fatally drawn to them.

Playing inside the line

Recently, a new style of leave has become popular. Here, the batsman brings the bat down away from the ball but still keeps it inside the line of the ball (17). To use this 'shot' requires great judgement and patience – knowing which balls to leave and which to play. Marcus Trescothick, shown on the left, proved to be a master of both – in his Test debut against the West Indies he didn't get his first run for nearly an hour, and played a lot of this kind of 'shot'. Nick Knight (one of Trescothick's rivals for a place as an opener) shows less good judgement (18), being tempted to play at a ball wide of off stump and so risk getting an edge and being caught in the slips.

Dropping your hands

Michael Atherton is a skilful exponent of a third method of leaving a ball. If a ball bounces or moves away unexpectedly, he jerks the bat down towards the ground, letting the ball pass over or wide of the bat. Often it looks as if the batsman has actually tried to hit the ball and there are a few 'oohs' from the crowd when the ball whistles past the edge, but actually he's in full control.

ATHERTON – IN CONTROL
This ball has bounced and moved away. By jerking the hands and bat downwards he has avoided contact.

Forward Defence

Obviously if the ball is straight a shot is required (and, anyway, you can't score runs by leaving the ball). You'll soon hear commentators rabbiting on about 'footwork' – the basis of all good batting. 'If you don't get your feet in the right position,' someone will be proclaiming, 'then you can't play the correct shot.' There's a bit more scope than that, but the basic principles generally hold true. If the ball is full, it's best to move forward; if the ball is short, it's better to step back.

To a straight, fullish delivery, the old fashioned adage was 'get forward and smother the ball' as exemplified in exaggerated style by the great Jack Hobbs (20) of Surrey and England.

It worked for him but it is impossible to lunge forward to that extent against 6ft 6in pacemen, or you will soon be wearing one on the chin. So, different times, different tactics.

JACK HOBBS C.1930
This position looks extraordinary to us now but it was designed for a different style of bowling. But don't knock it, he made 197 first-class centuries.

MICHAEL ATHERTON 2000
Against pace, the furthest forward you can hope to get is a half-stride. This confident block is classic MCC coaching manual.

THE BLOCK
Hussain's body is in a good position here, with his weight forward. He has moved confidently towards the ball.

THE HESITATION
Hussain is rattled, having just taken a blow on the fingers, and now he is not far enough forward.

Uncertain footwork

The mental battle of cricket is at its most intense during the opening overs of an innings. The batsman needs to exude confidence in the face of the bowlers hostility.

The pose of Nasser Hussain in the two pictures above seems little altered, but the small loss of faith they reveal is the difference beween being in and out. The picture on the left (22) shows Hussain solidly blocking a well pitched up ball from Courtney Walsh – he steps forward with a confident stride, getting well out of the crease. Annoyed by this kind of block, Walsh bowled a brute of a delivery to follow, which lifted and rapped Hussain on the hand.

After a pause for treatment (Hussain is known in the Essex dressing room as 'popadom fingers' because of their susceptiblity to breaking), he once again had to face the pace of Walsh.

Walsh pitched the ball up again but Hussain wasn't quite so confident this time and didn't get himself or his weight as far forward as before. It doesn't look much, but it made all the difference. The ball moved a little, he was struck on the pad and given out lbw.

This is a classic example of a batsman's confidence, and consequently his footwork, being eroded by aggressive and cunning fast bowling.

Back Defence

Having found his radar, a quick bowler is soon likely to test an opening batsman with some shorter-pitched bowling. Not necessarily bouncers at his head, just deliveries that rise up a bit and explore his technique, reactions and courage. Basically, if you are unhappy playing back, you won't get far as an opening batsman. The new ball will always bounce a bit higher than an old one, sometimes uncomfortably so.

Opening batsmen are forced onto the back foot pretty early by the extra bounce of the new ball. It's important they get on top of the bounce and try to keep it down, out of reach of close fielders. Sherwin Campbell uses literally every inch of space to do this, stepping perilously close to the stumps as he jabs the ball down. He's very chest on here, which, like Peter Willey on p.27, allows him to get his hands higher. The usual, orthodox stance on the back foot is more sideways on, with the hips aligned and pointing down the wicket.

Batsmen get a lot of hand jarring from fending off balls that ram into the top of the bat, and fingers. One technique called 'playing with soft hands' counters this by actually taking a hand off the bat at the moment of impact, this deadens the ball and stops it carrying to the slips (26, 27).

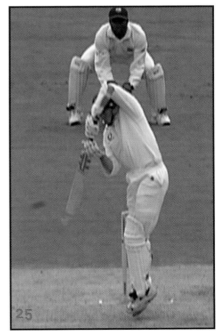

UNORTHODOX
Sherwin Campbell is using every inch of space behind him to get everything right behind the ball.

ORTHODOX
A traditional, sideways back defensive shot from Michael Atherton. He's got off his toes to get on top of the ball.

SOFT HANDS
Mark Ramprakash does the instinctive thing and takes his bottom hand off the bat. It is a risky strategy but is well executed here.

DEAD BAT
Atherton here is playing with very soft hands, and he has angled the ball wide of the slips to the boundary.

Footwork

You need to be nimble on the back foot, which is why most of the best batsmen in the world have been small and compact. Batsmen with larger frames tend to have slightly static footwork and get discomforted by quick, short bowling. The danger here is that the batsman gets tucked up into an awkward position and has to play jerky defensive shots, or as he instinctively moves out of the way of the ball actually takes his eye off it – with painful results.

GETTING LIFT
Tall, fast bowlers like Curtly Ambrose get a lot of lift. Luckily, this ball is outside off stump and is negotiable.

NOWHERE TO HIDE
Here, Graeme Hick is facing a ball that is just a bit straighter and there is just no option, he has to take it on the ribs.

Playing the Ball Late

The best batsmen in the world have the edge over their less talented peers in one other area – their instinctive skill and judgement allows them to delay their response to a ball a split second longer. Atherton is particularly outstanding at playing the ball late, which usually allows him to be in a better position and to play a better shot. While it can sometimes cause his downfall because he is *too* late on the ball, it saves him on many other occasions.

Here are two virtually identical balls, but Michael Vaughan (30) has planted his front foot down fractionally early. His head leans outside the line, he overbalances slightly as the ball moves in towards the pads and he is out lbw (see p.18). Atherton (31) delays his footwork momentarily, stays balanced on the crease and, as the ball nips inwards, it comes on to the bat – a piece of phenomenal judgement.

MICHAEL VAUGHAN
Although a good defensive player, Vaughan sometimes plants his front foot early and overbalances to the offside if the ball moves inwards.

MICHAEL ATHERTON
The fraction of a second longer that Atherton waits before committing himself ensures his weight is going forward rather than across the crease.

Top Test Batsmen

These are the real achievers in Test cricket. Not all of them are 'great' players, but all have made themselves indispensable by sheer consistency. Top of the tree Alan Border was no great stylist, but he was the rock of Australia for 16 years. Steve Waugh has inherited that mantle and is also amazingly consistent. Three other players deserve a mention: Gary Sobers because never mind making over 8,000 runs, he was also a dynamic bowler who took 235 wickets; Wally Hammond, who maintained an exceptional average of 58 through three decades; and the phenomenal Donald Bradman, who was out for nought in his last Test innings, which deprived him of 7,000 runs and an average of a hundred.

Batsmen with over 7,000 Test Match Runs

	Tests	Innings	Not Outs	Runs	Highest Score	Average
A R Border (Aus)	156	265	44	11,174	205	50.56
S M Gavaskar (Ind)	125	214	16	10,122	236	51.12
G A Gooch (Eng)	118	215	6	8,900	333	42.58
Javed Miandad (Pak)	124	189	21	8,832	280	52.57
S R Waugh (Aus)	132	210	39	8,722	200	51.00
I V A Richards (WI)	121	182	12	8,540	291	50.23
D I Gower (Eng)	117	204	18	8,231	215	44.25
G Boycott (Eng)	108	193	23	8,114	246	47.72
G St A Sobers (WI)	93	160	21	8,032	365	57.78
M C Cowdrey (Eng)	114	188	15	7,624	182	44.06
C G Greenidge (WI)	108	185	16	7,558	226	44.72
M A Taylor (Aus)	104	186	13	7,525	334	43.49
C H Lloyd (WI)	110	175	14	7,515	242	46.67
D L Haynes (WI)	116	202	25	7,487	184	42.29
D C Boon (Aus)	107	190	20	7,422	200	43.65
M A Atherton (Eng)	105	193	7	7,280	185	39.13
W R Hammond (Eng)	85	140	16	7,249	336	58.45
G S Chappell (Aus)	87	151	19	7,110	247	53.86
D G Bradman (Aus)	52	80	10	6,996	334	99.94

Attack

Once the batsman has gained a bit of confidence and is seeing the ball well, he can start to think about being more aggressive. There is, after all, not a lot of point in being out there for hours without making any runs. Because the new ball is liable to 'deviate' more, most opening batters bide their time, picking up most of their runs in nudges and pushes until at least lunchtime, eschewing the big shots. Their main objective is to blunt the new ball, not cane it to all parts of the ground.

However, not all openers share this view. Players like Australia's Michael Slater believe if it's there to hit, hit it, irrespective of whether it's the first over of the match or the 101st. He believes in asserting his authority immediately. His ferocious square cut to the boundary off Philip Defreitas's first ball of the 1994/5 Ashes was thought to have set the tone for the series (Australia won it 3-1).

On the front foot

Most openers are pretty circumspect though, content to plod along at two runs an over and just wait for any-thing slightly overpitched that they can punch back past the bowler. The straight drive (32) is a key shot here, it can be played with minimal foot-work but you need to use the full face of the bat. This is a low-risk shot based on timing rather than power.

If the ball pitches a bit wider, it allows the batsman to step out and play an off-drive (33). If the ball's swinging and darting around, the batsman will probably avoid playing this shot until he feels he's well in. In the meantime, he will leave anything wide and try to force the bowler to bowl straight.

STRAIGHT DRIVE
Although Trescothick hasn't got his whole weight forward, his hands bring the bat through perfectly straight.

OFF-DRIVE
The classic position: head over the line, elbow up, front knee bent and the full face of the bat in contact with the ball.

OFF THE TOES
The leg-stump half volley is bread and butter to the best batsmen. Little effort is needed to clip it away to the fence.

Patience, patience

The bowler, feeling put under pressure by the batsman, might eventually lose his line and bowl on the leg stump, allowing the batsman to clip it away for an easy four. Often at Test level an opening batsman has to wait a long time for such luxuries, but with a player such as Atherton his patience frequently outlasts the bowler's. His heroic 100 in the 2000 Test at the Oval lasted almost eight hours and featured 277 deliveries he didn't score from.

The West Indian opener Sherwin Campbell is less convincing when the ball is full. He is a player who tends to take a big step back as the bowler bowls, so he rarely gets his weight forward for the front-foot drive and ends up playing it away from his body, slicing the ball. Below, you can see he is leaning back and reaching out for the ball and so is not in control of the shot. His wrists twist, the ball flies off at an angle and he is often out caught in the gully.

OPENING THE FACE
Compare the position of Sherwin Campbell with Atherton (33). Campbell is leaning back, his foot is nowhere near the line of the ball and the bat face twists open in his hands because he's reaching for the ball. It could go anywhere.

Attack – On the Back Foot

If you can't play forcing shots off the back foot, you'll never make a Test opener. You don't have to be blazing away with hooks and cuts all day, but you do have to be able to nudge the ball away off your hip and play the odd back-foot drive.

The cut

The cut is probably the most commonly-used shot in the game. It is particularly favoured by small, compact players who haven't got much 'reach' for drives and other forward shots. However, to a ball that is widish and shortish, they can jump back on their stumps in a jiffy and bring the bat down like an axe.

The cut is certainly where Sherwin Campbell comes into his own. His usual batting position means he is already well back on his stumps most of the time, so in a perfect position to put anything away that is wide and short outside the off stump. The sequence below (36) shows Caddick's first ball of the 2000 Lords Test and Campbell was quick to show who was boss. Look at the final flourish and how close he is to the stumps when he completes the shot. The ball flew to the boundary head high, giving the batsman a strong feeling of one-upmanship. Significantly, after this Caddick was not at his best and Campbell made a rapid 82.

SQUARE CUT
Small batsmen are often very strong cutters because they tend to take a step back as the bowler releases.

Sherwin Campbell does this in the second picture, and therefore can seize on anything fractionally short.

TOO TIGHT
This ball is marginally too close to the stumps to cut. Trescothick has to lean back to hit the ball and still edges it (37).

MORE SPACE
Here the ball is wider and Trescothick gets his whole body over the shot and middles it for four (38).

Judging width

Left-handers love to cut. They get lots of opportunities because the natural angle of a right-arm bowler takes the ball across them towards the slips. But their judgement of width must be spot on. If the ball is fractionally too straight, it might get them into trouble. This is illustrated above, the first ball from Walsh (37) pitched a couple of inches straighter than the later one (38). In (37) Trescothick was cramped for room to play the cut shot and had to lean back slightly. He got a top edge which was dropped in the slips. Being a tad wider, the ball in (38) invited the cut and was dispatched for four. Being a cross-batted shot, the cut can be very productive but can also cause a batsman's downfall.

Atherton (not a left-hander) is a good cutter, but plays it in a more controlled way, making sure he's over the ball and hitting it down. Against top bowling you don't get many chances to play this shot. You need a trustworthy pitch (in this case the Oval) and must feel well 'in' (39).

PERFECT TIMING
This is one of Atherton's favourite shots, the controlled square cut, chopping down on a wide ball, hopefully sending it whistling through the covers.

The Pull and the Hook

There is a lot of confusion between the pull and the hook. Although they look quite similar, the basic difference is that the pull is played to a ball around waist height, the hook to a higher one at shoulder or head height, usually a bouncer. The hook is a harder shot to keep down (and safe) than the pull. Both shots have the effect of irritating the bowler and his response is likely to be venemous.

The pull

The pull is a back-foot shot with a hint of arrogance, since the ball's taken early, generally at arm's length in front of the batsman, and disptached through (or over) the leg side, often in front of square. It is a dismissive shot that says to the bowler 'is that the best that you can do?' and suggests the batsman is seeing the ball well. However, the batsman should then prepare himself for a bouncer. Atherton will tend to pull only on a very reliable pitch (you can easily come a cropper if the ball keeps low) or if he's played himself in. Because he tends to sit on the back foot, he's in a good initial position to play this shot to a shortish delivery rising to about rib height. As this ball (40) whizzed past short leg's left eardrum, it served the useful purpose of forcing him to retreat a bit out of Atherton's eye line.

THE PULL
A shot to a shortish ball that rises just above the waist and is dismissed past square leg, like a baseball shot. You must see the ball early to pull.

THE HOOK
The hook is an instinctive reaction to a higher rising short ball, the batsman helps it on its way by getting inside the line. It's a hard shot to keep down.

ENGLAND
1-1

CLANG!

Surprised by a quick, early bouncer, Nassar Hussain instinctively hooks, but the ball is too fast and straight and it clatters him on the head. This is a definitive example of what the West Indians call 'chin music'.

The hook

The most dramatic of all the back-foot shots (and therefore the most risky) is the 'hook'. Despite the dangers, some batsmen are compulsive hookers. As soon as they see the ball banged in very short they can't resist having a go at it. Nasser Hussain is one of these compulsives. Despite the fact that England are 1-1, he's still prepared to take on Walsh's bouncer (42). It's too early in his innings, the ball is still hard and new and aimed straight at his head. He can't get out of the way in time, and he takes a nasty crack on the head.

However, a bit later in the same innings a bouncer from Franklyn Rose wasn't quite so well directed. Veering down the leg side it doesn't lift as much either (43). Hussain gets inside it and latches onto it well, watching it all the way onto the bat, and then off it to the square leg boundary.

THWACK!

The emphatic nature of this shot will make the batsman feel he's on top of the bowling, and the bowler will feel that he mustn't drop short again.

MIDDLE-ORDER
BATTING

The batsman in the middle order has to be versatile – able to deal with various possibilities. He might be coming in on an easy pitch to exploit a dominant situation – able to give full reign to forceful stroke play. Equally, he may be fending off marauding bowlers on a minefield of a pitch, hemmed in by close fielders. The middle-order batsmen will be the most fluid stroke players but it goes without saying that in order to be effective their defensive play has to be secure.

A Waiting Game

You might assume that looking at the batting order of a team you would start with the best batsman and work your way down. That is not really the case – the best batsmen come in in the middle order. The opening batsmen, who have their own unique abilities, should have taken the venom out of the new ball and the edge off the bowler's aggression allowing the middle-order batsmen to come in and build a score. It is the great batsmen that come in at number 3 or 4, against a ball that has lost its shine, who can make batting look so effortless.

Facing all-comers

Out in the field, with the ball getting older and softer, it is harder to take wickets and so the fielding side will probably go on the defensive. Fielders will be moved back to save runs with a few close fielders kept up just in case. Patience is the key – for batsmen, bowlers, and spectators. There is a bit of cat and mouse going on, waiting for someone to make a mistake. Bowling changes will be a bit more frequent, trying to break the batsman's concentration. Batsmen will meet in the middle to talk strategy, observe that a certain bowler is looking a bit tired or discuss where they're having dinner tonight. The batsmen, having got their eye in against the pacemen, will then have to face whatever other bowlers the opposition have up their sleeves – from mainstream spin bowlers to the more unorthodox occasional bowler brought on for an over or two to confuse and confound. Playing spin bowling requires a different approach, and there are some batsmen who find it a difficult skill to acquire. Being nimble on your feet is crucial, getting to the pitch of the ball and perhaps disconcerting the bowler by charging him occasionally.

TAKING EVERY CHANCE
Middle-order batsmen need to be opportunists, biding their time but prepared to be positive. They will be the players with the dashing strokes and, hopefully, the big averages.

The Field

Test cricket is, like chess, largely a game of patience and, if no wickets have fallen for a while, the fielding side will generally go on the defensive and wait for the batsman to make a mistake. The field settings will reflect this, trying to plug gaps, dry up runs and frustrate the batsman into doing something rash.

A usual field setting for the middle order is the one shown below (2). It won't be as attacking as the field that confronted the openers in the first few overs (p.22). It is primarily designed to slow down run scoring. There are now only two slips, the other has gone to third man (a) to prevent thick edges or deliberate steers through the slips going for four. Cover point is still there (b). Silly point has retreated to extra cover (c) and the gully to mid-off (d). Pre-twentieth century, 'third man' was a close position next to the wicket-keeper and first slip, and meant literally 'third man up'. In the modern era, it's a boundary position used to slow the scoring.

It's always a dilemma for the captain whether to keep the gully (or third slip) in for one more over, in the hope that the bowler might induce an edge, or move him back to the third-man boundary. Sod's law dictates that, as soon as he takes out the gully (or slip), a ball flies at catchable height just where he would have been. At this stage, there will normally be three men on the leg-side: a mid-on (e), the short leg, who has moved to square leg near the umpire (f), and long leg (g). This is what's known as a 6-3 field (six on the off-side, three on the leg-side) and the bowler is expected to concentrate on and around the off stump, in the corridor of uncertainty (p.83) so as not to give away runs.

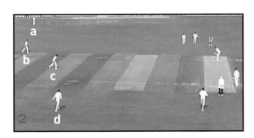

CONVENTIONAL 6-3 FIELD
These pictures combine to show a 6-3 field for a fast bowler, typical of the middle of an innings. Five men saving one, two on the boundary at long leg and third man, but two slips still stand guard.

KEY	
a third man	e mid-on
b cover point	f square leg
c extra cover	g long leg
d mid-off	

Maintaining Momentum

Now, run scoring is a bit harder. The bowlers might not be especially penetrative, the second-string ones may be on now, but they'll have found their length and direction and the field has been set to thwart the batsmen's favourite shots. Brute power, excellent timing and good placement of shots are needed to keep the scoreboard ticking over.

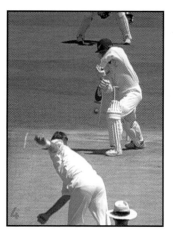

PUSHED DRIVE
This is a pushed drive (4) – note the higher bounce of the ball than in the regular off-drive (p.36).

FULL-BLOODED DRIVE
This is a real full-blooded drive 'on the up' (5) possible because the ball was a decent length but quite wide.

Hitting 'on the up'

If the bowling is of a consistent length (p.48) some balls might have to be hit 'on the up'. This is a drive to a ball that has pitched about four yards in front of the batsman, which is hit when the ball is almost at the top of its bounce, i.e. on the (way) up.

On the left is the New Zealander Nathan Astle about to drill a perfectly respectable ball from Andy Caddick back past the bowler (4). The ball is hit higher off the ground than the normal off-drive, and because of that it's harder to keep down and can really only be played on flat wickets. It is a difficult shot to play, so it often looks special

when it comes off. The batsman certainly feels the hairs stand up on the back of his neck.

On the right this thrash 'on the up' by Atherton to a widish ball from Nixon McClean is a collector's item (5). It is rare enough that a West Indian fast bowler offers a morsel this tasty, but Atherton even more rarely accepts the bait. This was played after Atherton had finally fought off the relentless double menace of Ambrose and Walsh and the relief is almost tangible. It's a fantastic shot with a free swing of the bat followed by a satisfying thud as the ball is whacked into the advertising hoardings. A batsman will be salivating over this sort of shot for months.

Opening the Face

Another option for batsmen trying to pierce a well set, defensive field is to angle the ball into the gaps. The technique of 'opening the face', which can cause an early-order batsman's downfall (because the new ball deviates more and is liable to catch the edge), can be valuable at this stage to manoeuvre the ball around.

Brian Lara is brilliant at this. With his Babe Ruth backlift (6), he generates exceptional bat speed, and then with flexible wrists, the bat face turns on the point of contact and carves the ball into space. A strong bottom (lower) hand helps guide the ball in the desired direction. It might look dangerous, presenting only half a bat to the ball, but the best players turn the wrist so late (almost as the ball is on the bat face) there is very little risk. Also, in Lara's case he hits the ball with such ferocity that even an edge takes some catching.

GETTING READY
This is the key to Lara's great power – no other batsman lifts his bat so high. But getting the bat this high means he also has to be exceptionally quick.

PRECISE STEERING
Despite minimal footwork, Lara's bat is right on line and, with a late turn of the wrists, he guides the ball into a gap.

STEALING RUNS

Lara's exceptional ability extends to manufacturing runs off good balls – this one was straight and bouncy, but he still glided it away from the field.

On the back foot

Lara is so versatile that he often opens the face off the back foot too. This is more of a defensive push, but he's still attempting to steer the ball away from fielders. Because of Lara's tendency to open the face, there will be more men posted square of the wicket than there might be to other players. It doesn't necessarily help. Lara's wrists are so strong and his eye so quick that he can hit the ball to all points of the compass. It is what makes him so entertaining.

OFF-SIDE   LEG-SIDE

SCORING ZONES

This is the kind of batsman's scorechart you'll see on Channel 4 showing where a particular right-hander scores runs.

Reading a scorechart

Lara has a right-handed team-mate, Sherwin Campbell, who also likes to open the face and score runs by slicing the ball through square. This is quite a controlled shot, angled through the covers. If you know that this is a batsman's favourite shot you can set the field accordingly. You will see on the scorechart above (9) most of his runs have been scored in an area square and behind square of the wicket on the off side. This is due to his rather loose driving. He hardly ever hits the ball straight, meaning there is not much need for fielders close to the bowler on either side. Opposing teams will know these traits and try to allow for them. More men will be stationed in the cover-point area and even behind square on the off side, and the bowlers will be advised to keep the ball fullish and not give him any width outside off stump.

What's it all About? - Length

While the line of a particular delivery determines where it is hit, the 'length' generally dictates whether it is hittable in the first place. For a bowler of any speed, fast or slow, a good length ball is one they hope won't be scored off (particularly if it's straight) because it's not full enough to drive or short enough to pull or cut.

a. Good length ball – from a fastish bowler, this will pitch five or six yards in front of the batsman, leaving him unsure whether to play back or forward. For a slow bowler it will be further up, perhaps two yards in front of the batsman.

b. Short of a length – this will pitch say eight yards from the batsman and force him onto the back foot. If it's a quick delivery he might have to fend it off his ribs; if it lacks venom it's likely to be pulled or cut.

c. A half volley – from a fast bowler this will land roughly two yards from the batsman. It's easier to drive this delivery because bat contact will be made closer to the pitch of the ball; it won't bounce up as much or have time to deviate.

d. A bouncer – this lands about halfway down the track, though the taller and faster the bowler, the closer it will be pitched to the batsman. A long hop is a bouncer that hasn't quite come off – the ball sits up at a good hittable height.

Closing the Face

To find gaps on the leg side, players 'close the face'. Again this is done with late movement of the wrists. Just as the ball makes contact with bat, the bottom hand turns the blade inwards guiding the ball away at right angles. It looks as if they're playing across the line, but they're not.

It seems that frail-looking batsmen of Indian origin are particularly good at this. Here's one, the left-handed Guyanese Shivnarine Chanderpaul, 'working' an off-side ball to leg (11). The ball was bowled on the side of the wicket where most of the fielders were but was hit to the side where most of them weren't. Occasionally, closing the face results in a 'leading edge' when the blade is turned too early, and the ball lobs up off the front edge of the bat. But with a last second flick of the wrists, it can be a most effective way of batting. The former Indian captain Mohammed Azharuddin was perhaps the consummate master of this.

You can usually tell if a batsman will tend to open or close the face by looking at how he holds the bat in

WRISTWORK
A last-moment flick of the wrists turned this ball from outside the left-handers off stump through the leg-side.

his stance. Chanderpaul (12) clearly has the bat turned inwards in his stance, implying that he'll be prone to hitting the ball on the leg-side. Jimmy Adams is the opposite (13), and prefers squeezing the ball out on the off side. You can set fields accordingly.

CLOSED FACE
Chanderpaul's blade is turned inwards (12) – the bowlers and fielders can see he is looking to play to leg.

OPEN FACE
Jimmy Adams stands with an open face (13). His favourite area for runs is a slice through gully.

Shot Selection

The key to successful middle-order batting is to be positive. This means not being lulled into defensive mode by restrictive bowling and field settings. It is important to remain watchful but ready to attack the bowler's slightest lapse in line or length.

PUNCHED DRIVE
A trademark Thorpe stroke, played with the full-face and very little follow-through.

Graham Thorpe on form is a good example of a positive middle-order player. He has a compact defence but is quick to seize on anything that is hittable. With a high back-lift, he restricts himself to three main scoring avenues: the off drive (14), the slash/cut (15) and the pull (16), which is more of a help-it-on-its-way shot. Each is played with an efficient punch rather than an over-dramatic flourish. He doesn't waste energy.

SQUARE SLASH
Thorpe waits for anything wide, indulging in the old adage, 'if you're going to slash, slash hard'.

Playing to your strengths

Thorpe knows exactly where he's hitting the ball. It may sound a bit limited to only have three major shots, but if you can play all of them well, against any type of bowling, there's no real need for any more. The batsman who has every shot in the book may ultimately be spoilt for choice. The clever thing about Thorpe is that once he's pushed the field back with a few fierce attacking shots, he dabs the ball into gaps and picks up lots of ones and twos.

FLICK PULL
Very quick on to anything short, Thorpe will take the fastest bowlers on and often succeed.

He is not what you would call a pretty player, but he is mighty effective and can adjust his game to the situation.

Running Between the Wickets

Good communication with your batting partner is something you're taught in the under-elevens and promptly forget when you turn professional. Taking quick singles is a basic discipline that, surprisingly, you keep having to remind Test players about.

It was brought to the forefront of the English players' attention by Duncan Fletcher, England's coach, during the 2000 West Indies series. Against the robotically accurate fast bowling of Ambrose and Walsh, the tip-and-run approach was very effective, keeping the scoreboard ticking over, rotating the strike and infuriating the bowlers at the same time. On several occasions it also provoked some wild throws at the stumps from the fielders, resulting in overthrows.

Keeping alert

Good 'backing up' and understanding from the non-striker is the key. An alert partner at the non-striker's end should be a stride up the pitch as the bowler releases the ball, ready to dart down the other end if the ball finds a gap. In the example (17) below, Michael Vaughan is well poised to run, leaning forward while just keeping his bat in touch with the crease until the ball has been delivered. (Note how far back Alec Stewart steps as the ball is released, which is what makes him such a fine back foot player, but occasionally vulnerable to being lbw.) On the right (18), the non-striker is well behind the line as Gough delivers the ball. This is lazy backing up, which could forfeit a run or put this batsman in danger at the other end.

AGGRESSIVE BACKING UP
Michael Vaughan is on the verge of leaving his crease as the bowler bowls, looking out eagerly for singles.

LAZY BACKING UP
Here, the non-striking batsman is well inside his crease and on his heels. From here he will find a quick single difficult.

Playing Spin

Historically, English batsmen have always been weak against good spin bowling. They just don't see enough of it. Quality foreign spinners like Shane Warne or Pakistan's Saqlain Mushtaq take hatfulls of wickets in county cricket, and whenever a good spin merchant has visited England post-war, he's generally tied the batsmen in knots (19). Few seem to have the skill to last for long. Seamer-friendly wickets up and down the country and spin-shy captaincy have not helped. Those who've batted on the Indian sub-continent seem better acquainted with what's required.

Playing yourself in

There is no doubt that the longer you hang around against spin, the easier it will become. Time in the middle, getting used to the spin and bounce and the bowler's variations, works wonders. A decisive defence helps, either getting the bat right out in front of the pad but still playing the ball as late as possible, actually feeling the ball onto the bat, or hiding the bat completely behind the pad as Atherton is here (20). It looks as if he's making no attempt to hit this ball and therefore is risking being given out lbw, but in practice few umpires are brave enough to argue that the batsman is not playing a shot. It's certainly a decisive method if not a very positive one. Batsmen get into trouble against spin when their approach is either kamikaze, or unsure. Those who are searching for the ball, and desperately lunging at it at the last moment with 'hard hands' don't last long.

GONE
Another lbw victory for Shane Warne, a batsman pinned on the back foot when he should have been forward. This shot captures the all-out competitiveness the Australians bring to cricket.

SOUND DEFENCE
Batsmen will hide their bat behind the pad when defending against spin.

The Top Twenty Test Batsmen

These PricewaterhouseCoopers (PwC) ratings are generally regarded as the best yardstick of a current player. The thing is, they take more than averages into account. Points are scored for the standard of the opposition, the state of the game and the quality of the pitch. For instance, runs made in a low scoring match count more than those made in batsmen-friendly conditions. Also more credit is given to a player's recent performances than to those earlier in his career. The ratings in February 2001, more than confirm the Indian master Sachin Tendulkar's ascendency over Brian Lara as the best batsman in the world, and Steve Waugh as the most durable player in the modern game.

PwC World Ratings: Top 20 Current Test Batsmen

		Rating	Average	Career best
1.	Sachin Tendulkar (Ind)	875	57.29	880 vs South Africa, Mumbai 2000
2.	Steve Waugh (Aus)	862	51.01	909 vs West Indies, Melbourne 1996
3.	Andy Flower (Zim)	831	51.06	831 vs India, Nagpur 2000
4.	Inzamam-ul-Haq (Pak)	801	46.22	865 vs England, Lord's 1996
5.	Ricky Ponting (Aus)	771	46.70	829 vs India, Sydney 2000
6.	Saeed Anwar (Pak)	767	46.31	835 vs India, Calcutta 1999
7.	Michael Atherton (Eng)	749	39.14	771 vs South Africa, Joburg 1995
8.	Rahul Dravid (Ind)	749	53.58	862 vs New Zealand, Hamilton 1999
9.	Brian Lara (WI)	748	48.29	917 vs Australia, St John's 1999
10.	Adam Gilchrist (Aus)	720	54.38	720 vs West Indies, Sydney 2001
11.	Mahela Jayawardene (SL)	715	41.86	748 vs South Africa, Durban 2000
12.	Daryll Cullinan (SA)	710	43.56	752 vs Sri Lanka, Galle 2000
13.	Michael Slater (Aus)	707	44.43	768 vs Sri Lanka, Melbourne 1995
14.	Jacques Kallis (SA)	703	42.62	764 vs Sri Lanka, Kandy 2000
15.	Yousuf Youhana (Pak)	699	40.30	699 vs England, Karachi 2000
16.	Gary Kirsten (SA)	698	41.80	766 vs India, Calcutta 1996
17.	Justin Langer (Aus)	694	39.61	767 vs New Zealand, Hamilton 2000
18.	Mark Waugh (Aus)	679	42.01	803 vs West Indies, Port-of-Spain 1997
19.	Chris Cairns (NZ)	677	32,56	705 vs Zimbabwe, Harare 2000
20.	Craig McMillan (NZ)	672	41.89	713 vs Zimbabwe, Bulawayo 2000

Using your Feet

You can't just block a high-class Test spinner all day, of course. The bowler gets into an unshakeable rhythm and, with close-fielders hovering around the bat like vultures, it's only a matter of time before a ball pops or spins sharply and loops up off bat or glove into one of their hands.

There are a number of ways to disrupt the spinner's rhythm, one of which is for the batsman to 'use his feet'. As Michael Atherton says, 'You must have a game plan before going to the crease. The key is in trying to play with quick precise footwork, and getting into a good position early, back or forward, but to be instinctive too.'

Generally, using your feet is a premeditated thing. The batsman will decide as the bowler turns at the end of his short run that this will be the ball he is going to come down the wicket to. The vital thing is that he doesn't telegraph his intentions and come too early. If the bowler has any suspicion that the batsman is going to give him the charge, he'll bowl it faster, or shorter or wider to foil the attempt. The batsman has to be very quick on his feet.

Getting to the pitch

In using his feet, the batsman is not only attempting to disturb the spinner's web, but also trying to get to the pitch. His aim is not necessarily to heave the ball into the road, but perhaps to drive it, or just to nudge it, into a gap. Mark Ramprakash gets into a good position here to do what

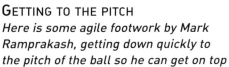

GETTING TO THE PITCH
Here is some agile footwork by Mark Ramprakash, getting down quickly to the pitch of the ball so he can get on top of the drive. A few advances like this from a confident-looking batsman will soon get rid of the close fielders.

CHARGE
Brian Lara is here charging Robert Croft. Croft probably saw him coming and dropped the ball shorter. Lara leant back and hit it for six.

he wants with the ball, which has pitched just in front of him (21), and is able to keep the shot down. The effect it has is to make the bowler wonder when he's going to do it again, and whether to therefore adjust his length. It gives him something to think about.

Charging the bowling

Often, you'll find a really good destroyer of spin, such as Mike Gatting, or Pakistan's Inzamam ul Haq, who charge the bowler one ball, and then, predicting that the bowler will drop the next one shorter, take a deliberate step back for the next one. Gatting used to 'mock charge', making a big initial movement as the bowler was about to release, pretending that he was going to use his feet, and then laying back on the stumps as the ball was delivered. There's a lot of cat and mouse going on when a spinner's operating.

Getting in position

There is, of course, a degree of risk in using your feet to a spinner, especially if you fail to get to the pitch. There is a real danger that the

ball will spin past the outside edge leaving the batsman stranded. If he has gone down the wicket and realises he's in trouble, he then has two options: get everything in the way of the ball and scramble back into his crease, or go through with an attempted big hit.

Brian Lara chose the second option against this Robert Croft delivery (23). Shimmying down the wicket when the ball was already in the air, he quickly realised he wouldn't be able to get down far enough to be on top of the ball, so leant back and let fly. He was secure in the knowledge that Croft had no protection (i.e. deep fielders) behind him so that even a reasonable mis-hit would land safely. In fact he middled it perfectly, and the ball landed in the 10th row. This majestic shot had a number of side effects. It made the batsman feel ecstatic, the bowler downcast and the silly-point fielder retreated to a safe distance. Two boundary patrollers were posted straight, leaving gaps either side of the bowler. Lara could now pick off easy singles by stroking the ball down the ground.

Sweeping

One of England's greatest post-war batsmen, the late Denis Compton, was once asked if he'd have gone down the pitch to the leg spin of Shane Warne. 'I don't think so,' he replied, 'he's got so many different tricks and he'd have seen me coming. I'd see how I got on sweeping him.' This seems to be the primary response of many modern English batsmen. They're afraid to use their feet against spinners for fear of being left stranded down the pitch and they rely heavily on the sweep shot. Since the advent of one-day cricket, with its cross-batted improvisations, the sweep has really been in vogue, though some batsmen naturally play it better than others and a few can't play it at all.

Beware the umpire

There is a degree of risk in sweeping: it is a largely premeditated shot and you're hitting across the line. There are strong possibilities of getting top edges, being bowled behind your legs or given out lbw. (It can look ugly if you miss the ball, and some umpires are notorious for judging a batsman lbw for 'the shot' – they don't seem to approve of the sweep for some reason.) On the other hand, it can bring a lot of runs. A good sweeper can totally frustrate a bowler and confound their field settings. Alan Knott could sweep anything, even a high full toss, and could place the shot exactly. Graham Gooch destroyed the Indian attack with the sweep in the 1987 World Cup. He used a range of sweeping styles, from the paddle – a dinky little flick-shot that sends the ball wide of the keeper with the bat virtually on the floor – to the slog-sweep, a big muscular heave over mid-wicket.

FINE SWEEP
Nasser Hussain can sweep the ball firmly or delicately (as here) making sure he gets low down to the ball and rolls the wrists to keep the stroke down.

LEFT-ARM SPINNER'S FIELD
Here, there are three men in the covers, a deep square leg (out of shot) and a gap at mid-wicket.

KEY			
a	short extra cover	**c**	mid on
b	short fine leg	**d**	silly point

Piercing the field

Executed well, the sweep pierces the normal left arm spinner's field (25), which is off side-biased. There are two close catchers, a few men in the ring and a boundary fielder (not shown). Driving is risky because of the man at short extra cover (a) but, because there are only three men on the leg-side, there's usually a gap beside the square-leg umpire. A sweep should produce at least one run, although there will be a man stationed deeper on this line, to prevent the boundary. Also note the presence of the short fine leg (b), to stop the paddle, and catch the top-edged sweep. Against non-sweepers you won't see anyone in this position.

Hussain, however, can sweep from almost any line. This one (26), from the New Zealand left-arm spinner Daniel Vettori, is around off stump. Hussain's pad covers the wicket so, should he miss the ball, he has a second line of protection and is unlikely to get out. He has played it well here, by getting out to the ball and rolling his wrists to keep the shot down. Spinners are happy to see batsmen doing this if there is any turn about, they know there is a lot that can go wrong with it. The ball can bounce up and flick the glove, slide off the inside edge onto the stumps or fly off the top edge into the batsman's face. For sweep-happy batsmen, wearing a helmet and visor is vital.

PLACEMENT
Hussain is a prodigious sweeper, placing the ball away from the fielders. However, there is a danger of a top edge into the face.

The Reverse Sweep

If the orthodox sweep is partially premeditated, the much-maligned reverse sweep is wholly so. Because you have to adjust your grip somewhat, once you've decided to play it, it's virtually impossible to bale out. Although it was first exhibited by the Pakistani Mushtaq Mohammed in the 1970s, reverse sweeping is largely a recent one-day cricket phenomenon, played mainly to foil negative leg-stump spin bowling and/or stereotyped field settings. It's called a reverse sweep because it is hit on the opposite side to a normal sweep.

You don't see it that often in the Test arena, and even less often from a left-hander, but Chris Scofield, England's precocious young all-rounder, unveiled it in his first Test innings. The extent to which reverse sweeping is hugely premeditated (and therefore often scorned by the purists) is amply demonstrated here.

In the top shot (27), the batsman is thinking about playing an orthodox sweep, but if the ball isn't suitable he can still abort and reach out to block it. But in the bottom sequence he has already inverted the blade in readiness for playing the reverse sweep. There's no going back from this point, with the bat and wrists pointing the wrong way. Luckily, the ball was in the slot and he swept it past the wicket-keeper's left hand to the boundary. It's a huge fillip for the batsman if the shot comes off.

However, it can be disastrous. England captain, Mike Gatting, played the reverse sweep to Allan Border's first ball in the 1987 World Cup final and edged it to the keeper. England's run chase bit the dust, and he wasn't forgiven for a long time.

NO GOING BACK
Top is the orthodox sweep (27). In the reverse sweep (28) the back of the bat faces the bowler as the ball is released.

Playing with the Spin

Although sweeping is probably the most popular shot against spinners, it is certainly not the safest. Hitting straight is the least risky option. In fact, that goes for any bowling. Against spin, though, it's sometimes necessary to adjust the straightness of your shot at the last moment. This is achieved by turning the wrists in the direction of the likely spin as the ball is about to make contact with the bat. This is a delicate skill known as 'playing with the spin'.

Only a few players can master it, and it tends to be those who play the ball late. It helps to have almost rubbery wrists, which Shivnarine Chanderpaul definitely does (see p.49). You can just see below(29) how Chanderpaul prepares to hit the off-spin of Croft (spinning away from the left-hander) straight back past the bowler. But as he sees the ball spin, his wrists twist outwards, and the blade of the bat turns towards the cover fielders. You can tell by these two stills, separated only by a fraction of a second, how quick you need to be. If the bat had continued down a straight line, the ball would have probably taken (or passed) the edge. By opening the face, Chanderpaul has effectively ridden the spin, and guided the ball to safety.

The Indian maestro Mohammed Azharuddin was a brilliant exponent of this skill; he was able to turn the blade in a flash to counter the spin. At times, his bat was whirring round so much it was like bowling at a revolving door.

RUBBERY WRISTS
Here, the batsman looks to drive the ball straight (left). However, he realises that the ball is spinning away from him, *which he deftly counters by turning the blade outwards and playing with the spin.*

Mastering the Spin

In Pakistan during the winter, Michael Atherton gave a masterclass in watching the ball right onto the bat and playing with the spin. They weren't big, dramatic shots and therefore they went largely unnoticed, by they did help him pick up singles, rotate the strike and keep the scoreboard ticking. This can be done off either the front foot or the back, as the sequences below illustrate.

The bowler, in this case Saqlain, is predominantly aiming outside off stump, trying to spin the ball into the batsman (30) in the direction of the arrow, left, keeping all the close fielders interested as Atherton plays a dead bat. Knowing there's a gap away to the right of shot, he rides the spin, turning the blade at the last moment, and just plonks the ball delicately into the unguarded area past mid-wicket (30, right). There's a high degree of difficulty in these shots (30 and 31) – if you turn the blade too early the ball may lob up for a catch.

Psychological victory

Little nudges and pushes into these available gaps intensely irritate the bowler, releasing the pressure he's trying to build up. Also, they force him to change his field. In this case, Atherton took so many singles playing with the spin in the square-leg area, Saqlain had to move his short leg away to plug the gap (32). It represented an important psychological victory for the batsman (shifting a close fielder) and was achieved with brain rather than brawn.

BACK FOOT
Waiting until the ball is under his nose, Atherton nurdles the turning ball into the leg side.

FRONT FOOT
Atherton gets out to the pitch of the off break and places the ball with the spin into the same gap.

Making Room

Because spinners bowl at a slower pace (between 50 and 60mph, compared to quick bowlers' 80+mph) there is more time for 'foot-work'. Another way of scoring runs off spinners is to hit them off the back foot. Their accuracy means you might have to manufacture yourself some space to hit the ball – instead of moving down the pitch, you step away from it slightly, making room to cut.

GETTING LOW
This is an excellent position to play the late cut, making room by getting the lower body out of the way.

WRONG CHOICE
Hussain made room here to attack this ball but it spun back and rapped him on the pad.

Michael Vaughan does well here (32) making room by leaning back to give himself the space to play the shot, while still keeping his head in line with the ball. He's just dabbing the ball backward of square, but you can play a full-blooded cut from this position too. Nasser Hussain, though good at this shot, chooses the wrong ball here (33). It was quite wide but then turned sharply back at him. Though he makes every effort to get his body and legs out of the way, the ball has tucked him up too much and grazes his pad, before being taken by the wicket-keeper. To make matters worse, he was wrongly given out caught.

Beating the spinners

Overall, balance, quick feet and expert reading of the length are vital when playing spin. Spinners will wheel away for hours trying to probe your weaknesses, hoping for a little bat-pad catch or a rush-of-blood heave. It's vital the batsman is patient and watchful but still ready to pick off any runs there are to be had. A spinner who is allowed to bowl maiden after maiden will soon start taking wickets. It doesn't have to be a hoik into the grandstand every over to upset his rhythm. Just little nudges and nurdles here and there will do the trick, and the four-ball will come along soon enough.

LATE-ORDER
BATTING

Tail-end batting is as much in the head as any other batting. The blokes at the bottom of the order might not have as much talent as their more stylish counterparts, but they can partly make up for that with guts, dedication and common sense. The fact is that everybody in the team has to bat (whereas not everybody has to bowl) so they might as well make as good a job of it as they can.

Winning the Match

The days when the quick bowlers could just slip a couple of straight yorkers under the crooked bats of the lower order are getting rarer. Tail-end batting, like other neglected areas of the game, is now the subject of both physical and mental coaching. The reason for this is that, in fact, tailenders often win Test matches. Teams that make 450 in the first innings rarely lose the game and more often than not they win it. And the opposite is generally true for teams that are dismissed for less than 250. Frequently, the difference lies in the contribution made by the last five batsmen – as opposed to the first five.

The most successful Test teams have taken this on board. In the process of achieving world domination, Australia, for example, frequently eked out an extra 200 runs from Ian Healy, their no.7, assisted by Shane Warne and the other bowlers following him. South Africa's lower order, featuring Shaun Pollock, Lance Klusener and Mark Boucher, were so consistently successful people often wondered why they didn't reverse the batting order.

Playing England, however, bowling attacks felt that they only had to get five out and the rest would fall down. When they took the field with Giddins, Tufnell and Mullally at The Oval in 1999, they were effectively playing with eight batsmen and three rabbits. It's one of the weaknesses

Duncan Fletcher addressed when he took over as England coach at the end of that year and in recent tests the English tail has shown a bit more confidence and grit.

The tail will have a mixture of styles and techniques, often not very orthodox. There will be those who want to swing at everything and those who only want to block. Some defensive ability, and the necessary concentration, is vital because often the time taken up by these last batsmen at the crease is as important to the balance of the game as any runs scored.

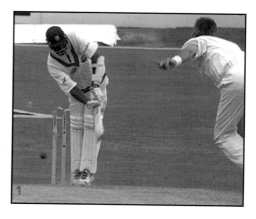

YORKED
The fate of many a tailender, yorked by a ball he just can't dig out. The departing batsman may be able to bowl a yorker but not play one.

Occupying the Crease

Late-order batting is largely a question of attitude. Glenn McGrath is generally reckoned to be one of the worst batsmen in the world, and his average of 5.84 (runs per innings) reflects that. But he works his butt off every time he goes to the wicket, using himself as a human shield to stop the ball getting through, frustrating the bowling side and allowing more able colleagues to add precious runs. It's is all part of the teamwork that has made Australia the hardest side to beat.

A tailender like McGrath might only have made half a dozen in a last wicket partnership of 35 but the time he's taken up is as vital as the runs that have been added. That annoying extra half-hour in the field can have a significant psychological effect, demoralising the fielding side and giving the batting one a real buzz that can dictate how the next hour's play goes.

There is a good incentive for tail-enders to hang around at the crease. They're under no pressure, as they're not expected to do much, so any extra runs are a bonus and will be received enthusiastically. Also, the ball is usually soft (unless the new one has just been taken) and the bowlers are weary – they've been out there a while. Even more importantly, a decent stay at the crease puts off the moment they have got to go out and bowl themselves. The flip-side is that their specialist job (bowling) is a very tiring one, and some just haven't got the energy, or mental discipline, to bat for long. That is why until recently England's no.6 batsman often ran out of partners.

Top Scoring Partnerships for the 10th Wicket (* not out)

151 – B F Hastings (110) & RO Collinge (68*) New Zealand v Pakistan, Auckland 1972–73

151 – Azhar Mahmood (128*) & Mushtaq Ahmed (59) Pakistan v South Africa, Rawalpindi 1997–98

133 – Wasim Raja (71) & Wasim Bari (60*) Pakistan v West Indies, Barbados 1976–77

130 – R E Foster (287) & W Rhodes (40*) England v Australia, Sydney 1903–04

128 – K Higgs (63) & J A Snow (59*) England v West Indies, The Oval 1966

127 – J M Taylor (108) & A A Mailey (46*) Australia v England, Sydney 1985–86

Rotating the strike

If the no.6 is still in, it's vital that 9, 10 and 11 try to stay there. They don't have to do anything clever. The longer they hold an end up, the more frustrated the bowlers will become. You'll probably see some unusual extremes in the field settings in this situation. Up-close and very personal for the tailender, trying to keep him on strike and swiftly remove him, or pushed back offering easy singles to the no.6, trying to get him off strike in the early part of an over. Then the field will close in for the last one or two balls, attempting to keep the decent batsman pinned down that end so that the other bowler can have the whole of the next over at his less accomplished partner.

Running between the wickets is therefore crucial for the tailenders, to ruin the fielding team's plans. Here Andrew Caddick, England's no.9 and a tailender who frequently sells his wicket dearly, is batting with Michael Vaughan, a recognised batsman (2). He is hemmed in by close fielders, as you'd expect facing the bowling of Curtly Ambrose. The West Indies know if Caddick faces the whole over there is a fair chance they'll get him out. England soon scupper that idea. Caddick gets tenaciously behind the ball, Vaughan is backing up aggressively and, as soon as the ball drops safely, he's haring up the wicket. It only goes perhaps five yards from the stumps but they're through for an easy single and Vaughan is back on strike. This was a valuable partnership on a difficult Headingley pitch and England's last five wickets really counted. The West Indies left the field so demoralised (and England so elated) they were shot out for 61.

EVERY ONE COUNTS
Andy Caddick, a tenacious tailender, exhibits a model forward defensive nudge and an alert response to his partner's call. It's frustrating for the bowler who hoped to have a whole over at Caddick.

Nightwatchman

Despite being England's resident no.9, Andy Caddick has a good orthodox batting technique – principally a resilient defence – making him the favoured choice as England's nightwatchman. This is an expendable player sent in late in the day, as the name suggests, to protect the specialist batsmen from fading light and prowling bowlers. If, for instance, there are ten overs left in the day and England, batting second, are 30-1, the next man in (the no.4) will probably request a nightwatchman be sent in if a wicket falls.

It is not the best job in the world. The nightwatchman is expected to 'farm the strike' (face as much of the bowling as possible) for the remainder of the day and is usually treated to a liberal diet of fast short-pitched deliveries that he is obliged to fend off his chest. Often the ball is still relatively new and hard and the bowlers fresh and revved up, so it's an uncomfortable experience, and the physio is on red alert with the cold spray. The nightwatchman has no licence to play any attacking shots and enjoy himself, as this is risky. Instead, he has got to defend stoically

and grin and bear it. The only plus is that if he survives the night, he has got scope to enjoy himself with the bat the following morning, and there have been a few cases when they really did. Alex Tudor's unbeaten 99 against New Zealand in 1999, won the match for England.

Old habits

Getting a nightwatchman padded up in the last half-hour of the day is common practice for Test teams. However, the Australian captain Steve Waugh has cast doubt on the practice recently, arguing that a specialist batsman avoiding going out to bat late in the day is almost a dereliction of duty, and not in the best interests of the team. He does have a point. Few nightwatchman are technically equipped to deal with the hostility directed at them, and often the ploy backfires, obliging the top order player to come in anyway, and another wicket has gone down. But old habits die hard and again, it can have a psychological impact. If the nightwatchman can manage to hang on well into the next morning, the fielding side can get very demoralised.

TAKING THE KNOCKS
This is a typical experience for a nightwatchman. He will receive a lot of short deliveries if he hangs around for long and a few bruises for his trouble.

Protect Yourself

Because they are inferior batsmen, tailenders usually wear all the protective equipment they can lay their hands on. This is wise as there is no such thing as the fast-bowler's union and if they hang around for long, their appreciation of 'chin music' will be checked out to the full. They don't get much protection from umpires these days either. However, being padded up to the eyeballs causes other problems – once the batting team have been bowled out, there's not much time to get ready to take the field.

Quick change

Only ten minutes are allowed between innings (just enough time for the pitch to be rolled) and then it's on with the action again. This can make for some funny sights as the teams come into the pavilion. First in are the opening batsmen from the fielding side who for the last half-hour have been pre-occupied with how they will play the first ball when they bat. They now have about five minutes to don batting trousers, pads, box, thigh pad, inner-thigh pad, arm guard, chest pad, helmet, inners and gloves.

The opening batsmen are quickly followed by the dismissed batsmen, one of whom is probably due to open the bowling in eight minutes' time. This is almost a worse predicament. Darren Gough picks up the story: 'I have got to get upstairs, undo all my batting gear, get my damp shirt off and socks off, put dry ones on, get a clean jock strap on, get my bowling trousers on, get the suncream on and lace up my boots. Then I realise I've forgotten my ankle brace, so I have to take off my boots and trousers again to get it on.' Not surprisingly, he's usually last out of the dressing room hurriedly tucking his shirt in and zipping up his flies.

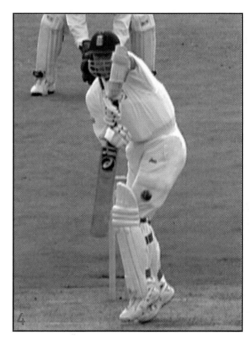

MAXIMUM PROTECTION
Darren Gough, well padded to face the West Indies. He's got an arm guard, two thigh pads and a chest pad. As the last batsman, he won't have much time to get it off before going out to bowl.

BOWLING WITH A
NEW BALL

Opening bowlers are, literally, the giants of cricket – huge, tall men with a killer instinct. They will emerge at the start of play, fired-up, looking for first blood; the batsmen facing have to be confident and calm. The opening bowlers have the most physical job in cricket; you can't project a cricket ball down a pitch at 90mph without expending a huge effort. However, the best are also tacticians, knowing when to tempt and when to torture a batsman.

The Pacemen

The fast bowlers (they are the ones who are always given the new ball) will have listened to the captain's challenge: 'get early wickets, and don't let them get off to a flier'. It is the usual fast-bowler's lot. Somehow, he must bust a gut to take wickets without giving runs away. That's never easy with fielders clustered round the bat. Two wickets in his first spell (six or seven overs) would be good, three ideal. He might, if things are going well, bowl throughout a whole session (about thirteen overs on the trot).

However, things may conspire against him – the pitch may be unresponsive, slip catches could go down, suddenly the score is 50-0 and the opening bowler is retiring to the boundary, feeling demoralised.

The decision as to which bowler bowls from which end will have been made. The senior (or faster) bowler will get preference, and will usually opt to bowl with the wind. If it's a cross breeze, he'll choose the end where the wind will help his natural movement. It is very useful to have a pair of opening bowlers who move the ball in opposite directions so that they can both benefit from the breeze.

Fast bowling is very much an individual skill – all you ask from your team-mates is that they are alert to every chance. These are the players most prone to injury because the strain on their bodies is enormous. Courtney Walsh, the world's leading wicket-taker, has a relatively easy, fluid action and has remained remarkably injury free, but many a fast bowler's body has buckled under the strain.

A Test team without at least two big pace men seems a very toothless attack. Pace dominates, and with it has come improved helmets, gloves and padding of all sorts, to protect the batsman from the onslaught.

FIRST BALL
Everyone is ready and waiting – the bowler is looking for something to happen early on, he needs to get the psychological advantage from the start.

Run-up

How many times have you seen a fast bowler carefully pace out his run, place the marker at his starting point, then charge in and bowl a rearing express delivery, only for it to be called a no-ball because he has over-stepped the crease? There are two obvious reasons for this: nervous over-enthusiasm, or poor run-up measurement.

The run-up is actually one of the most neglected areas of the fast-bowler's technique. Few take the trouble to mark it out accurately, relying on a number of giant strides, which are bound to vary in length from day to day making the end point wildly variable. It would make far more sense to work out their run-up in practice, measure it exactly with a tape measure and then mark it out precisely before the game, allowing a few inches for over-excitement if their tails up.

No-balling

No-balling is generally a product of an inconsistent run-up and it can be a real annoyance. The delivery doesn't count (effectively it's a free hit, although against quick bowlers there is no time to change the shot after hearing the umpire's call), and it can throw the bowler's rhythm. His run-up totally determines his balance and momentum as he arrives at the wicket. If the run-up is too fast, he will overbalance in delivery; if he's no-balling, he'll start to run in slower

'The run-up is one of the most neglected areas of a fast bowler's technique'

NO BALL!
Curtly Ambrose over-stepping by quite some margin. A no-ball counts one to the score and has to be re-bowled.

and he'll be 'reaching' for the line and leaning back. If he's worried about overstepping, for instance, he will slow as he approaches the wicket, disrupting his stride and take-off point. It happened consistently to the West Indian Reon King during the summer of 2000, and he bowled terribly. In the end, he couldn't seem to remember which foot to start off with.

Speed

Interestingly, Allan Donald discovered that the more smoothly he approached the crease, the faster and better he bowled. If he charged in, he seemed to lose both speed and direction. As a result, his coach, Bob Woolmer, used to time his run-up to the millisecond to find the optimum speed. It was one of the reasons Donald wore an ear-piece on the field during the 1999 World Cup (until it was outlawed) so that Woolmer could advise him whether to speed up or slow down

his run. The variety of run-up approaches, from Holding's glide to Marshall's gallop, is one of Test cricket's delights.

Length

The length of the run is governed by what feels natural. Generally, the taller the bowler, the further he'll need to run to get going, but over-rates (and over-rate fines) have to be weighed against the desire to charge in from the sightscreen. At roughly the length of a pitch (22 yards), Dominic Cork's run-up (3) is about average. You can see his mark, which he will try to land on when he's about three strides in to his run. Run-ups seem to have got shorter in recent times, although Pakistan's Shoaib Akthar is a distinguished and mesmerising exception.

Action – Coil and Spring

There is perpetual argument about what makes a good fast bowler's action. One thing's for sure, the explosiveness of fast bowling puts a lot of strain on your body however you let go of the ball. It is generally agreed, however, that you can divide all good actions into two categories: front-on and side-on.

Side-on delivery

This is the textbook technique and Darren Gough's action (4) is classically side-on. Just prior to delivery, Gough's front arm points roughly in the direction of the batsman and he looks over his left shoulder at the wicket with his chest facing the non-striker. His left foot will be pointing at (right-handers) long leg and he will pivot off it as he releases. Side-on bowlers tend to be plagued with frequent injuries.

Front-on delivery

Courtney Walsh is a fine example of the alternative, front-on method (5). It's very typical of the loose-limbed, West-Indian style. In mid-air, his left arm is pointing towards the off-side and he looks under his left shoulder. His chest is facing down the wicket (it's sometimes called an open-chested action) and as he lands, his front foot will be pointing towards the slips. It's a very relaxed, easy style, and, as Walsh is the leading

DARREN GOUGH – SIDE ON
This is the MCC approved bowling action but propelling the ball like this is not a natural movement and can lead to injuries.

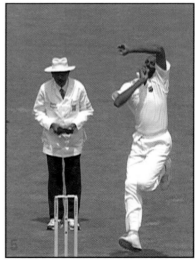

COURTNEY WALSH – FRONT ON
You can see that Walsh's action is a smooth fluid one, everything is moving in the same direction.

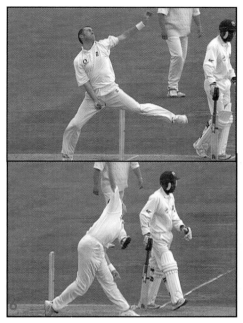

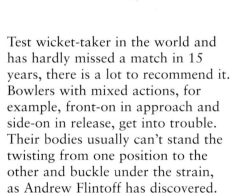

Craig White

Craig White's is an explosive action – his front leg is braced as he lands, making sure he maximises height.

Dominic Cork

Dominic Cork's action lacks the impact of White's. His knee is bent as he delivers the ball and so he loses a bit of height.

Test wicket-taker in the world and has hardly missed a match in 15 years, there is a lot to recommend it. Bowlers with mixed actions, for example, front-on in approach and side-on in release, get into trouble. Their bodies usually can't stand the twisting from one position to the other and buckle under the strain, as Andrew Flintoff has discovered.

Achieving momentum

Each quick bowler uses his body in a slightly different way, which accounts for why some are quicker than others. Gough is a strong, bustling sort of bowler, Walsh is more loose-limbed and languid. Allan Donald's form is a combination of supreme athleticism

and timing. Height is obviously important but there are lots of other factors. The examples above are viewed from side-on, and clearly show why two men of similar physique bowl at quite different speeds. The left sequence (6) shows Craig White, who has surprised people with his consistent pace of above 85mph, with a big delivery stride and a muscular coil, rather like a javelin thrower. That and his explosive release bear quite a resemblance to Jeff Thomson (see p.74). It is immediately obvious from these pictures that Dominic Cork's gather and pivot (7) lack the range and power of White's, which is why his average speed is around 75mph.

The Great Actions

Watching the actions of different bowlers is fascinating because there is a bewildering variety of ways of getting the ball from A to B. Each one in this galaxy of stars has their own idiosyncratic style. However, they all have something in common (apart from at least 200 Test wickets each), their heads are all almost perfectly upright, eyes level, when they release the ball, which suggests balance is as important as brawn.

LILLEE
Denis Lillee shows menace, versatility and sheer pace from a classic side-on action.

THOMPSON
Jeff Thompson, with the spring of a young sapling, regularly slung balls at over 90mph.

HOLDING
Michael Holding made the uprooting of stumps look effortless.

MARSHALL
Malcolm Marhsall was quite slight but, charging to the wicket (chest-on), he generated great pace.

KHAN
Imran Khan's giant leap and explosive release was one of cricket's great sights.

HADLEE
Richard Hadlee combined precision and merciless efficiency – he scalped 431 Test batsmen.

WALSH
Courtney Walsh is the master of disguise and the world's leading Test wicket-taker.

Top Test Bowlers

Courtney Walsh, Mr Duracell himself, dominates this list. It's no coincidence that to take by far the most wickets he has bowled the most overs. The West Indians Malcolm Marshall and Curtly Ambrose are the only men to take their wickets at a cost of under 21. The other phenomenal performers in this list are Richard Hadlee, who carried the New Zealand attack for at least a decade, and Ian Botham, who quite apart from his prodigious haul of wickets also made fourteen Test centuries with the bat.

There are three spinners in the list. Shane Warne – whose 366 wickets at a relatively cheap cost is amazing. Lance Gibbs was another prodigious wicket taker, and Mattiah Muralitharan, who, at 29, is almost bound to become the leading Test wicket taker of all time.

Bowlers with 300 Test Wickets

	Tests	Overs	Runs	Wickets	Average
C A Walsh (WI)	127	4.739.3	12,193	494	24.68
Kapil Dev (Ind)	131	4.623.3	12,867	434	29.64
R J Hadlee (NZ)	86	3,653.0	9,612	431	22.30
Wasim Akram (Pak)	100	3,662.1	9,478	409	23.17
C E L Ambrose (WI)	98	3,676.4	8,503	405	20.99
I T Botham (Eng)	102	3,635.5	10,878	383	28.40
M D Marshall (WI)	81	2,930.4	7,876	376	20.94
S K Warne (Aus)	84	3,917.1	9,505	366	25.96
Imran Khan (Pak)	88	3,243.0	8,258	362	22.81
D K Lillee (Aus)	70	3,077.5	8,493	355	23.92
R G D Willis (Eng)	90	2,892.5	8,190	325	25.20
Waqar Younis (Pak)	68	2,203.0	7,046	313	22.51
L R Gibbs (WI)	79	4,519.1	8,989	309	29.09
G D McGrath (Aus)	67	2,662.1	6,817	309	22.06
A A Donald (SA)	65	2,359	6,679	311	21.47
F S Trueman (Eng)	67	2,529.4	6,625	307	21.57
M Muralitharan (SL)	59	3,145.4	7,704	303	25.42

Extra Bounce

It is an increasing trend for fast bowlers to be tall. Harold Larwood, the original 'Bodyline' bowler, was only 5ft 9in and great bowlers from the 50s and 60s like Ray Lindwall and Brian Statham, among others, were barely 6ft. Malcolm Marshall was only 5ft 10in, which makes his achievement of taking 376 Test wickets at the rapid strike rate of one every 46 balls all the more amazing. Now, the majority of quick bowlers are well above average height, with Curtly Ambrose at 6ft 8in towering over everyone.

Bowling from these elevations, the ball is liable to bounce more, and be awkward for the batsman to keep down. Also, it's harder for him to see. He has to look up at the bowler's hand, which is often well above the level of the sightscreen, then suddenly finds the ball rearing up at his face.

Maximising height

Bowlers don't always make full use of their height but Andy Caddick (15) is renowned for the steep bounce he gets out of any pitch. Clearly he maximises his 6ft 5in height by keeping his head upright

in delivery and, most importantly, bowling over a braced front leg. He gets a lot of extra power, and therefore speed, from this rock-solid position. He's pivoting off his front leg, and getting real momentum from it. Alan Mullally (16) is the same height as Caddick but as he lands at the crease, his front leg bends and his whole body buckles slightly, meaning he's not bowling from as rigid or as lofty a position. Although he's an accurate bowler, Mullally doesn't always seem to get as much as he could out of a pitch, both in terms of lift and venom.

Andy Caddick
Andy Caddick exploits every inch of his height (15) and so is able to get a high degree of bounce.

Alan Mullally
The explanation for Mullally's lack of real penetration is clear from his action (16) – he is not making the most of his physique.

Movement off the Pitch

Opening bowlers will always begin by gripping and releasing the ball 'seam-up'. It is the conventional method to try to get deviation when the ball is in the air (known as swing) and off the pitch (referred to as seam). The ball's seam acts as a rudder when it's in the air, facilitating swing, and as a ridge when it hits the pitch, accentuating seam. Therefore, it's common policy to release the ball so that the seam stays upright in flight. There is no guarantee that it will deviate, of course, just by landing on the seam. That will depend on pitch conditions – for example, whether the pitch is damp, green or cracked. Also, the bowler has no idea which way the ball will go. But then, the advantage is, neither does the batsman.

Seam

Courtney Walsh is regarded as a seam bowler, since he relies more on movement off the pitch than in the air. Below, you can see his normal release (17) where he is attempting to get the ball to land on the seam and hopefully 'jag' one way or the other. Although Walsh has an unusually fluid wrist action, he has no real control over which way the ball will go. But as the angle of the seam is tilted slightly, it would normally move from right to left. This (to a right-hander) is a 'leg cutter'. This term has nothing to do with possible injury (although a good leg cutter can seriously damage your average) but is derived from the fact that it cuts from leg to off.

SEAM UP
Courtney Walsh has a supple wrist action – he appears to give the ball the faintest tweak from right to left while still keeping the seam upright.

Leg cutter

This sequence shows a great example of a dramatic Walsh leg cutter (18). The ball pitches around the line of the off-stump. At this point the batsman and bowler have no idea which way the ball is going to move, or indeed if it's going to move at all. If anything, because Walsh bowls from wide of the crease, the batsman might have expected it would be slanting towards leg stump and he could shape up to play it to mid-on. In fact, the ball hits an irregularity on the pitch and jumps so far to the batsman's right, Michael Vaughan could barely have hit it with a stable door never mind a bat. It's a delivery Walsh has produced time and time again in his career.

Sometimes a ball like this is referred to as a 'jaffa' or a 'peach' – meaning an unplayable delivery. Nobody is quite sure how either of these terms originated, but if you get one, you've just got to pray that it's not straight. The irony is that it is the ball that moves an inch, rather than a foot, that usually takes the wicket.

LEG CUTTER
Here are three stages of an unplayable delivery. The arrow shows just how dramatically the ball changes direction. The problem with facing this type of bowling is not knowing from one ball to the next how great the movement off the pitch will be.

Movement in the Air

Swing bowling is an incredibly fragile art. Some bowlers seem to have the action and aptitude to achieve it, others don't. Even those who can, find that there are days when they can't. Some new balls swing and others don't. Even if I could, there is absolutely no point in trying to explain why swing happens. Thousands of scientists have had a go and, while all their efforts are admirable, they seem to end up just confusing each other and everybody else. What is certain is that a shiny cricket ball does swing – the amount depends on the conditions, the bowler and the ball itself.

19

Outswing

Where Walsh is more of a seam bowler, Darren Gough – with his lower, slingier action – is more of a swing bowler. He bowls predominantly outswing to the right-hander (also known as away swing), this is when the ball veers to the left). He will release the ball seam-up and aim it at the right-hander's off stump, on a fullish length, hoping that it will curve away from the bat and take the edge (or better still, bowl him). This is a classic example (19), with the ball angling in towards the stumps. It starts to 'bend' late in flight and finishes up six inches outside the off stump. Because it all happens so quickly, the batsman is drawn towards the ball. It grazes the edge and he is caught at second slip. The batsman's lack of foot movement didn't help him.

LATE SWING
Darren Gough makes a new ball curve away from the batsman in the air and take the edge. It's skilful bowling but the batsman will be annoyed that he got drawn in to the shot.

Bowling to left-handers

The outswinger to the right-hander can be equally lethal to left-handers (20). The batsman above, is deceived into thinking that this ball is a juicy half volley he can drive comfortably to the fence. The swing seems only to take effect in the second half of the ball's journey and, to the batsman's horror, it ducks in past his flailing bat and rearranges his furniture. All he would know about this dismissal is the deathly clatter of ball on stump, and then the long walk back.

THROUGH THE GATE

The outswinger becomes a lethal inswinger to the left-hander, ducking between bat and pad.

Scrambling the seam

Andrew Caddick also bowls outswing, but uses a clever variation to confuse the batsman. His normal delivery, held seam-up, swings away from right-handers (22). But releasing the ball with a scrambled seam stops it swinging (23). Instead, it angles into the right-hander and across the left-hander towards the slips (21).

PAST THE EDGE

The left-hander here (Warell Hinds) is expecting this ball from Caddick to swing in, but it's a scrambled seam delivery and it veers the other way.

GOOD VARIATIONS

Caddick's two releases, viewed from the batsman's position. The outswinger is released seam-up (22) unlike the scrambled seam delivery (23).

Attacking Fields

An opening bowler, in fact any bowler, should have the main say in what field to set, since he knows best where he's going to bowl. They'll have done their homework. They'll know, for instance, that Michael Atherton is predominantly a back-foot player, so they'll be looking to pitch the ball up and drag him forward, where he's less comfortable. A player who's predominantly a front-foot lunger, may well be confronted by several short legs, because he tends to be uncomfortable against the short ball. A happy-hooker may find a man put back at deep square leg.

Slips and gullies

An outswing bowler like Darren Gough or Dominic Cork will concentrate on a strong slip cordon (24), with protective fielders straight on either side, because he'll be attempting to pitch the ball up and try to make it move away (see arrow). This is appropriate bowling from the Nursery end at Lord's because the pitch slopes downwards from right to left as you look at the pavilion – the slope aids the bowler's movement. Sometimes, if the ball is really bending away from the batsman, an outswing bowler will try operating to a 7-2 field (7 on the off-side), reinforcing the slip cordon (25). Despite the amount of movement, it's a hard field to bowl to. The batsman is constantly looking for anything straight that he can knock into the vacant leg-side areas, forcing the bowler to readjust his line outside the off-stump, allowing the batsman to leave most balls alone.

24

6-3 FIELD
A typical setting for an away-swing bowler early in an innings (24). Six on the off-side and three on the leg (long leg is out of view).

7-2 FIELD
Because the ball is swinging away, the bowler can afford an extra man in the slip cordon (25).

25

Probing the edge

The opening bowler's number one priority is to make the batsman play. What batsmen love are several friendly overs that they can watch whistle harmlessly by, with the odd four-ball thrown in. What they hate is remorseless accuracy and lots of searching deliveries that they're not sure whether to play or leave. Incite indecision in a batsman and you're over halfway to getting him out. That's why the best new ball bowlers use the bouncer only sparingly. Not only might it sail harmlessly over the batsman's head, but it also expends energy, which ought to be directed at this point into the 'corridor of uncertainty'. It's Geoff Boycott's favourite phrase and the batsman's least favourite place. Basically, it's a channel on the pitch about eight inches wide, on, and just outside, the off-stump. Especially when facing a new ball, which can swing or deviate either way off the pitch, batsmen aren't sure what to do with balls landing in this channel (26), indicated here by two parallel lines. Play at a ball in this area and it might dart away and take the edge. Leave it and it might nip back and rattle into the pads or, worse still, uproot the stump. It's a dilemma that the batsman has about 0.38 seconds to resolve. Only a few rare pacemen can stick at it for long – of current bowlers, Glen McGrath sticks at it the longest.

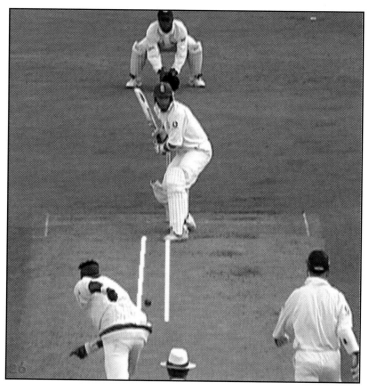

IN THE CORRIDOR
Curtly Ambrose has been a master of landing the ball consistently in this channel. He can do it ball after ball, which means his bowling poses a constant threat.

Shock Tactics

Some new-ball bowlers just aren't able (or willing) to patiently stalk the corridor of uncertainty. They'd sooner blast the batsman out than smoke him out. They'll try to bowl as fast as they can and vary their length and line, often more by accident than design. In amongst the odd good length delivery will be a sprinkling of bouncers and yorkers meaning that the batsman has to stay on red alert.

'CHIN MUSIC'
Courtney Walsh is the supreme exponent of 'chin music' – this sequence illustrates it perfectly. It means that the helmet is now an essential part of a batsman's protection.

Bouncers

It is with good reason that the bouncer is the most feared delivery in cricket. Propelled somewhere near the middle of the pitch, it's aimed to rise up towards the batsman's jaw and make life uncomfortable for him. A batsman who is a compulsive hooker or doesn't seem to line up the bouncer too well, will be peppered with them (although only two per over are allowed in Test cricket).

Walsh is a corridor-type bowler, but he will suddenly unleash a surprise bouncer. The ball will be banged in half-way down the pitch and much quicker than his regular delivery (27, top). His head and leading shoulder dip down fractionally more for this ball, but it's all too quick for the batsman to see. In this instance, it definitely was for Hussain. This one struck him on the head while he was still halfway through his stroke.

This type of bowling is exciting to watch because no one is quite sure what is going to happen next. One ball may be loose and smashed to the boundary, the next may be a snorter that singes the batsman's nostrils, leaving him watchful and hesitant.

Yorkers

The yorker is the other extreme attacking option. Instead of bouncing the ball at the batsman's upper body, it's an attempt to sneak it under his bat. The derivation of the term reflects this. In the nineteenth century 'to york' or 'put Yorkshire on' someone meant to cheat them or deceive them. Andy Caddick has done this brilliantly here, pitching his yorker (28) right on the batting crease (bowlers often focus on the base of the stumps when they bowl a yorker) before it crashes into the stumps. You might wonder, given this result, why fast bowlers don't bowl yorkers all the time. The fact is, there is little margin for error. If you get the length a few inches out it will be either a half volley or a full toss, and as likely as not will disappear to the boundary. Get the length right, though, and the batsman will need a shovel to dig it out.

'There is very little margin for error when you bowl a yorker'

YORKED
Having softened the batsman up with some short-pitched stuff, Andrew Caddick then kills him off with the ideal follow-up – the perfect yorker.

Left-arm Fast Bowlers

Batsmen don't see left-arm fast bowlers all that frequently, so having one to open the bowling is a priceless asset. Bowling from the other side of the stumps, he is coming at a different angle from the right-armer. He will therefore ask alternative questions and most batsmen feel they need to adjust their stance and guard. With no swing, his natural delivery, if pitched on the line of the stumps, will veer towards the slips. This is something the majority of batsmen just aren't used to.

Most left-arm pacemen can produce a ball angling across the right-hander. That's all very well, but if that's the only delivery a left-arm quickie can bowl, good batsmen will soon suss him out. They'll know that any ball pitched on line will veer towards the slips, missing the stumps and therefore not requiring a shot. The bowler, meanwhile, will have to land the ball outside the leg stump to hit the wicket, meaning he can't get an lbw (the batsman can't be out lbw if the ball pitches outside the leg stump). A few left-armers – notably Akram – can complement their natural angle with a ball that swings back into the right hander from an off-stump line. If they have this ball in their armoury, it makes them doubly effective. It immediately creates uncertainty. The batsman, not sure if a ball on off stump is the one veering across him or the one curving back into him, is obliged to offer a shot regardless.

WASIM AKRAM

A left-arm paceman's stock ball angles across the right-hander hoping to take the edge as indicated by the arrow above (29). Wasim Akram has taken many of his 400 Test wickets with this delivery. The best left-armers, can make a ball swing back into the right-handers as well (30).*

Variations in swing

These sequences show how difficult it is for batsmen to predict what a ball from a good left-arm bowler will do. The bowler is New Zealand's Shane O'Connor. He is that rare species, a pacy left-arm swing bowler (England's last equivalent was John Lever). The first sequence shows a ball to Atherton on a full length, around about the line of the off-stump (31). Atherton gets into a good position to counter the angle, but the ball swings back into him late, raps him on the pad and he's lucky to survive a big lbw shout (perhaps he was hit just outside the line). The second sequence shows a ball from O'Connor's next over, he pitches a ball on a similar line and length (perhaps a shade wider) to Nasser Hussain (32). Hussain, having seen O'Connor's late in-swing, prods circumspectly at the ball, expecting it to come in. Instead, possibly more by accident than design, it holds its line, takes the edge and Hussain is gone.

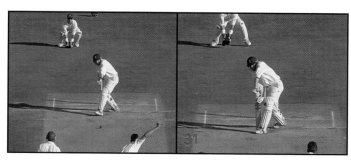

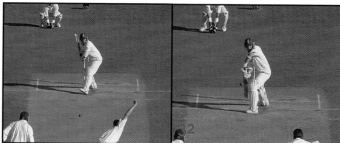

LEFT-ARM BOWLING
These are two examples of the problems left-arm pacemen can pose. Both these deliveries pitch roughly around off stump. The top one, to Atherton, swings back to get him almost lbw. The bottom one, to Hussain, goes straight on to take the edge and Hussain's wicket.

Hard work

So there's a lot more to opening the bowling than merely charging in with a new ball and hurling it down the other end as fast as possible. There are days and pitches when the quicker you bowl, the quicker the ball tends to fly off the bat. And, in the modern era, if things don't go right, you can't wander off to the long-leg boundary and peruse your navel for a few hours, occasionally putting out a cursory size 12 to stop the ball from going for four.

BOWLING WITH AN
OLDER BALL

'A few tight overs, please' or 'bore 'em to death' are common captain's requests with an older ball, and most will opt for this patient approach at first to try to regain the initiative. It's likelihood of success relies, in the main, on how long and effectively the bowlers can sustain it, and whether there's any response from the pitch. On the surface it can make for a rather turgid period of play, but in fact there is a lot of subtlety afoot.

Stepping up the Pressure

A second new ball isn't available until the 80th over, so the last 10-20 overs with the old ball are often at a critical point in the game. If the batting team have done well against the new ball, making a useful total, then a breakthrough is urgently required. Or, if the bowlers have been on top, it is important to keep the momentum going and not let things begin to slip away. The fielding side will probably still be relying more on pace than spin, but they need to employ a variety of strategies to make something happen.

The strategy will depend, by and large, on the state of the pitch, the weather and, indeed, the match. Using the patient approach – attempting to bowl tightly to frustrate the batsmen into doing something rash – might be fine in some circumstances but if the batting team are 140-3 chasing 200 to win in the fourth innings under sunny skies, urgent, remedial action is required.

The defensive option

Certain teams, denied a breakthrough, will just set the field back and try to bowl a series of maidens. The Australians are very good at this, particularly when Glenn McGrath is bowling. Frequently he'll bowl four or five straight balls, then finish the over with a high bouncer which is impossible to hit, ensuring the batsman stays runless for another over, and gradually the pressure builds up. The West Indians, with their battery of lanky pace bowlers, were also good at this in their heyday.

Here are two balls of a typical over from Curtly Ambrose, whose length and line are so repetitive, you wonder sometimes if he's a man or machine. I've drawn a small area on the pitch into which Ambrose landed every delivery in this particular over. It was clever bowling, because although each ball bounced in roughly the same spot, the vagaries of the pitch (Headingley) ensured that each one behaved differently.

AMAZING ACCURACY
Ambrose can drop ball after ball in the same spot. It doesn't mean all the balls are the same but it does mean the batsman knows he can't relax for a second.

Swing

On typically lush English grounds that protect the ball's condition, bowlers gradually develop a discernible sheen on one side of the ball. From about the tenth over onwards, they've decided which side to polish (perhaps one side has got a small scuff on it, therefore the other side will be preferred) and most fielders will give it a rub as they pass it back to the bowler. All this attention is in aid of swing. In normal conditions a ball with the shine on the right will veer left. With the shine on the left it will veer right – this is conventional swing.

As batting becomes easier against an older ball (it's often assumed the pitch has got easier, when actually it's the ball that has lost its hardness) swing comes into its own. The more highly polished a cricket ball is on one side, the more it seems to swing. (Bowlers often maintain a really shiny cricket ball in their bag to bend it round corners in the practice nets and give themselves more confidence.) Often one player is appointed a sort of chief-polisher. The slight canting of the ball's seam acts like a rudder to assist the change of course (3).

Not every bowler can make this work, and few can make a ball swing in two directions. It seems you need the right combination of bowling action, trajectory and release to get the ball to swing, and even then it doesn't always happen. Shining agents are sometimes surreptitiously applied to a ball – suncream for instance – although this is officially outlawed.

Weather conditions and also the ball itself can conspire against swing. There is a school of thinking that a cloudy, muggy day will enhance swing, but it is yet to be proved why this should be. Also, some bowlers swing the ball earlier in flight than others, making it easier for the batsman to sight and deal with. But there's no doubt, a bowler who can make the ball swing late, and at pace in most conditions, is worth his weight in gold. It is how Ian Botham achieved a hefty proportion of his 383 Test wickets.

 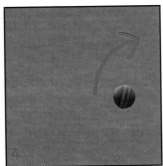

CONVENTIONAL SWING
Shine on the right will help the ball to swing left (3) – outswing to the right-hander. Shine on the left will help it to swing right (4) – inswing.

Reverse Swing

This term has entered cricket vernacular in the last decade and confused almost everyone. The concept is actually quite simple. On certain, usually dry surfaces, the ball becomes badly roughened on the side the bowlers aren't polishing. At some point, usually around the 40 over mark, it starts to swing in the opposite direction to conventional swing, i.e. with the shine on the right, the ball will swing right (the reverse of the norm). The shine can just be seen on the right-hand side of this delivery (5) and the ball curved to the right in line with the arrow.

Beyond science

It is hard to know why this happens, although scientists have speculated about things such as 'turbulent air layers'. Teams have their own idiosyncratic ways of exacerbating reverse swing, some legal, such as wetting one side and keeping the other dry, and some illegal, such as scratching the ball. What is known is that faster, slingier bowlers like Darren Gough, Craig White and Waqar Younis get more reverse swing, and it comes later in the ball's flight. It seems to help if the seam is tilted slightly in the direction of swing, the ball slicing through the air rather like a flying saucer. The sharp, dipping movement of reverse swing is dreaded by batsman but, until recently, it was only Pakistani fast bowlers who had perfected this art, regularly decimating lower orders with a series of lethal inswinging yorkers. Now others are catching on, and this dry-wicket skill is even eroding the role of spinners in some Test teams. It's increasingly widespread in England, particularly on cracked pitches at Lord's and Old Trafford.

IN REVERSE
Craig White has mastered the art of making an older ball with the shine on the right swing right – the opposite of conventional swing.

5

What's it all About?- Ball Tampering

Bowlers have fiddled with the ball for decades, picking or raising the seam, smothering it in vaseline, rubbing it with talcum powder. Anything to try to challenge the perceived dominance of the bat in test cricket and get the ball to swing or seam. It was technically illegal (you were only supposed to use sweat or saliva) and there was the odd bit of finger wagging from the umpire if it was spotted. Nothing, however, like the full blown scandal that exploded during the 1992 Pakistan tour of England. TV cameras caught a Pakistani bowler allegedly scratching the ball to try to get it to reverse swing. Having seen the ball curving round corners, various English players cried foul, an investigation was launched and the ball was impounded. No immediate action was taken but, from then on, umpires were ordered to inspect the ball at regular intervals, and the laws concerning unfair play were redrafted to stop teams rubbing balls on the ground, for instance.

The issue surfaced again after the famous 'dirt in the pocket' incident when Michael Atherton was caught on camera apparently sprinkling dust on the ball. There have been one or two other contraventions since, and Imran Khan threw in a grenade, claiming he had once scratched a ball with a bottle top and accusing other Test players, including Ian Botham, of ball tampering. Botham contested these allegations in the High Court. Imran won. Activities on the field are now well-policed and, for the time being, the subject has gone underground and been superseded by more serious issues. But just as car thieves always try to stay one step head of security systems, so bowlers will always strive to find new ways of getting through the batsman's guard.

WEAR AND TEAR
A new ball gets severely roughened during play in dry or dusty conditions, but bowlers are not allowed to hasten the wear and tear artificially.

Using the Crease

Some fast bowlers revel in bowling with an older ball – it gives them license to go through their repertoire of tricks. Darren Gough is one: 'I could bowl boringly and concede about 2 runs an over but that's not my way. I'm prepared to try anything – leg spinners, yorkers and slower balls to get wickets.' This is why Gough is usually successful, occasionally frustrating but always entertaining. He conjures wickets from nowhere with old-fashioned virtues like using the crease.

Here's a fine example of Gough's mercurial brilliance, from Headingley 2000. He had dismissed Brian Lara several times in the series and had just taken two quick wickets with late swing. The top sequence (7) shows him bowling from his normal position close to the stumps, attempting to swing the ball into Lara's pads. Lara just jammed down on it in time. For the next ball, he jumped out wider on the crease (8). Lara noticed this and assumed Gough was going to slant one across him towards the slips. Lara decided, on seeing its angle and line, to leave it alone. But this was still the inswinger. It swung in and had him plumb lbw.

INSWINGER
Gough bowls his standard inswinger to Lara from close to the stumps. Lara sees it and blocks it.

THE SWINDLE
The next ball is bowled from wide of the crease. Lara thinks it will veer across him and leaves it. But it too is an inswinger and he is out lbw.

Round the Wicket

By going 'round the wicket' a bowler can achieve a very dramatic angle change. Most bowlers start off delivering from 'over the wicket' (keeping the umpire to his right for a right-armer) but there's nothing to stop them trying the other side. At first, it's a bit disconcerting running in with the umpire to your left, and it's hard to stop running straight down the pitch in your follow-through. But it asks different questions of the batsman: for example, balls bowled from round the wicket come into a left-hand batsman rather than going across him.

The White angle

Craig White troubled all the West Indian left-handers with this line of attack in the summer of 2000 (9). The angle of delivery is hugely different from over the wicket. White managed to get the odd ball from here to slant in to the left-handers, and then swing away towards the slips – a very difficult ball to play. To cover this potential ball, Brian Lara goes across too far on his first ball at The Oval and loses his leg stump (10).

To right-handers, bowling round the wicket has value too, presenting the same sort of 'should-I-leave-should-I-play' problems as a left-arm over bowler like Wasim Akram might. Malcolm Marshall even used to run up behind the umpire before jumping out to let you have it from just beside the umpire's earlobe.

ROUND THE WICKET
Craig White poses angular problems bowling round the wicket (a) instead of over (b) to the West Indian left-handers.

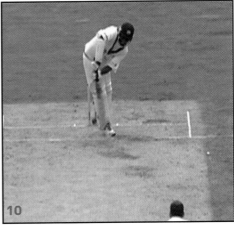

DECEPTIVE LINE
Lara went across too far for this White round-the-wicket delivery and lost his leg stump as a consequence.

Top 10 Strike Rates by Bowlers in Test Cricket

A bowler's strike rate is the number of balls he requires for every wicket taken, e.g. a strike rate of 60 means that, on average, a bowler takes a wicket every 60 balls (or 10 overs). In their prime, you'd certainly like every one of these demons in your world eleven. Waqar Younis is perhaps a surprise at the head of this list, but if you saw him at his peak in the early 1990s bowling 90mph banana-benders, you'd understand how he's been able to average a wicket every seven overs. He perpetually bowled at the stumps, working on the basis that 'if you miss, I hit'. A lot of people not only missed, they didn't manage to get their bat down at all. Of the others, Marshall's feat is a revelation, as much as anything because he was only 5ft 10in – very short for a pace bowler. Trueman's presence underlines that he could play a good game as well as talk one, and in the middle you have two of the legends of that great West Indies side of the 1970s and 1980s – Big Bird (Joel Garner) and Whispering Death (Michael Holding). Glenn McGrath, the unstinting Australian spearhead with the evil bouncer, may well still improve his already excellent strike rate.

Top Strike Rates	
BALLS PER WICKET:	
Waqar Younis (Pak)	42.23
M D Marshall (WI	46.76
F S Trueman (Eng)	49.43
R J Hadlee (NZ)	50.85
J Garner (WI)	50.85
M A Holding (WI)	50.92
G D McGrath (Aus)	51.69
D K Lillee (Aus)	52.01
J R Thompson (Aus)	52.67
R G D Willis (Eng)	53.40

Variations of Pace

As the ball gets softer and less shiny, it's generally going to be easier to score runs against. A good way of upsetting the batsman's rhythm and making timing his shots harder is for fast bowlers to vary their pace. Subtlety is vital. It isn't just a matter of ambling up to the wicket and turning your arm over more slowly. The batsman would see that a mile off. An element of disguise is required.

Sleight of hand

Slower balls have been around a long time, but the methods of concealment have improved considerably. Allan Donald's technique was typically modern. With his strength, co-ordination and fast arm he was the quickest bowler in the world for most of the 1990s, regularly capable of delivering balls at over 90mph. The ball on the left of this split sequence is his normal fast delivery (11). The wrist, hand and fingers are 'behind' the ball. But in (12) he is bringing his arm over at the same speed and cutting his wrist across the line of fire as if trying to spin the ball. The pace of the ball is reduced to about 70mph (which is still quite quick). The imparted spin also gives a bit of 'loop' to the ball.

Bit of a blur

It all happens so quickly that the change is almost invisible to the batsman. Often he doesn't realise until it's too late. The effect can be seen on the opposite page. The top sequence is Donald's quicker ball (13), which the batsman is able to judge and hits successfully. In (14) we see the slower ball and here the batsman plays too early. He is through his shot before the ball has arrived, overbalances and is bowled. It's a delicious swindle for the bowler.

DELIVERY STYLES
Donald's seam-up delivery (11) travels at around 90mph. By cutting his wrist across the ball (12) he immediately reduces this to around 70mph.

11

12

Getting the measure

The three shots at the bottom show how a good batsman learns to deal with changes of pace (15). On the left, Courtney Walsh's beautifully disguised slower ball (he just lets the ball flop out of his hand with a limp wrist) was so good that Graham Thorpe lost the ball completely. In fact he thought, because the ball seemed to loop higher, that it was travelling straight at his head. That's why he turned his back, only to suddenly feel the ball lobbing into his ankle. Gradually, as the summer of 2000 wore on, he got a little better at playing Walsh's slower ball. It still got him out lbw in the first innings at The Oval (15, centre) but by the second innings, the element of surprise had gone and Thorpe had the measure of it.

THE QUICKER BALL
Donald's quicker ball is just where the batsman expects it, though it hits high up the bat.

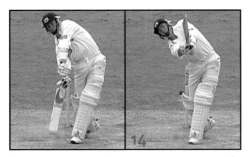

THE SLOWER BALL
Having negotiated the quick ball the batsman is deceived by the slower one, plays too early and is clean bowled.

However, once a batsman has been deceived by a slower ball, his suspicions are aroused and he's on the look out for it. He's preoccupied and so may miss scoring opportunities. This has a powerful influence in one-day cricket. Suddenly, he can't just heave at everything because he doesn't know how fast it's arriving. The Australian Ian Harvey is the best one-day bowler in the world, mainly because of a brilliant slower ball released undetectably from the back of the hand. Batsmen, hopelessly early on their shot, invariably ladle a simple catch back to the bowler.

EYE OFF THE BALL
Walsh's slower ball confounded Thorpe at Old Trafford. It flummoxed him once at the Oval too, but by the 2nd innings he'd sussed it.

The Element of Surprise

As the innings wears on with few wickets falling, you'll see other ploys being tried. The bowlers are rotated, fielders will be moved about, unorthodox positions deployed or sudden bouncers unleashed. Mike Brearley, England's most successful post-war captain, sometimes placed the fielding helmet close to the batsman to tempt him to aim a shot at it (and thereby collect five runs). But the practice was outlawed before it achieved anything and it must now be placed behind the wicket-keeper.

Setting the trap

If a batsman has a known penchant for the hook, he might be denied the shot for a while and then suddenly offered one to have a go at that is quicker and higher than he expects. Dominic Cork had a valuable success with this strategy against Sherwin Campbell. He probed away on a fullish length for several overs, drawing the batsman forward, then suddenly unleashed a high bouncer, which Campbell, who was well in, couldn't resist (16). The ball practically pitched on Cork's toe and got up so high that Campbell couldn't control the shot. He ended up flailing at it over enthusiastically and getting a top edge that flew straight into long-leg's hands. The batsman trudged off looking and feeling humiliated, but that takes the credit away from the bowler. It was an inspired effort from Cork, which disrupted the West Indian flow and saw their innings go into decline. A high bouncer is also sometimes used as a defensive tactic, the ball ballooning over the batsman's head and impossible to hit. It frustrates the batsman and makes him wonder when his next run is coming.

SURPRISE, SURPRISE
This is shrewd thinking from Dominic Cork, who suddenly delivers a very high bouncer to Sherwin Campbell, after a sequence of dot balls.

Sherwin Campbell, who is 80 odd not out, can't contain his excitement and lashes out at the ball, but he can only slice a catch to long leg and is gone.

The three-card trick

What was especially good about the Cork to Campbell ruse is that the bowler didn't telegraph it in any way. He just suddenly dished up a bouncer. The 'three-card trick' is the total opposite of this. Everything is signposted. The batsman should know exactly what to expect. This tactic is as old as the game. Like selling a defender a dummy, it still works. The first card is the surprise bouncer. Often the batsman's a bit startled by it, has a go at it anyway, but is about half an hour late with the shot (17). 'Oh, so you fancy a hook do you?' says the bowler's expression as he sends a man back towards the square-leg boundary to catch a possible mis-hook (18). The batsman, adrenaline pumping, starts thinking, 'Am I a good hooker, is the pitch reliable and, most importantly, will the next one be the bouncer or the bluff?' Nine times out of ten, it's the bluff, the pitched-up delivery, looking for the lbw. Here, sadly, Cork fell for it hook, line and sinker (19).

THE SURPRISE BOUNCER
Out of the blue, Cork gets a taste of his own medicine – a surprise bouncer. He doesn't see it at all and is hopelessly late on it.

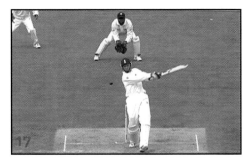

THE FIELD CHANGE
Seeing Cork having a go at the bouncer, the bowler sends a man back to deep square leg for the attempted hook shot.

THE BLUFF
It's all an elaborate decoy. The next ball is full. Cork, expecting the bouncer, is back on his stumps, rapped on the pads and palpably lbw.

SPIN BOWLING

Spin bowling is one of the most intriguing aspects of the game – the variations a good spinner can input on a ball defy explanation. Googlies, flippers, and chinamen are all part of the spin-bowler's armoury, and their names are as difficult to fathom as the balls are to play. It may be called slow bowling but this is not a gentle art – the great spinners bowl with aggression, cunning and surprising speed.

Reviving an Old Art

You don't have to be long at a cricket ground to hear someone mourning the dying art of spin bowling. They're usually the type of cricket fancier who also believe that helmets should be banned, as should any team that doesn't bowl 25 overs an hour. In fact, in world terms, spin is not dying at all, it is experiencing a renaissance. The English spin cupboard may be a little understocked at present, it is true, but elsewhere batsmen are regularly getting caught up in the sticky webs of Shane Warne, Anil Kumble, Mattiah Muralitharan and Saqlain Mushtaq, to name but four.

England rarely take to the field without at least one spinner, and the twirlers always have an influence towards the end of a home Test series. They are not there just for an exploratory over before tea. These days you will even see quick bowlers trying the odd spinner.

It is a fallacy to think that spinners prefer to bowl late in the day with a ragged, old ball you wouldn't give your dog. They like to get into the action with something hard that will bounce just as much as the pacemen do. And, like the pacemen, they are often aggressive in words and deeds. Bringing on a spinner early is actually quite a bright idea, because top-order batsmen are not so used to slow bowling and, with a new ball, some spinning deliveries might grip and turn and others, pitching on the shiny part of the ball, might skid straight on.

If the seamers are finding assistance from dampness in the pitch then the spinners may benefit as well. Having a quick bowler at one end and a spinner at the other is also a good ploy, although, as a spinner gets through his overs in two minutes flat, it can start to leave his huffing, puffing partner rather short of breath.

FULL ON
Shane Warne brought new passion to the appeal, almost ordering umpires to give batsmen out.

Off-spin

Off-spin, a traditional skill – turning the ball from off to leg (left to right) – has produced the greatest bowling figures in the history of the game, Jim Laker's 19-90 against Australia at Old Trafford in 1956. It was a damp, sticky pitch, before the advent of covered, drier wickets and the increasing use of the pad in defence, both of which have rather negated the impact of off-spin. However, the recent emergence of the big-spinning Muralitharan and the deceptive Saqlain has breathed new life into the art. More of that later.

The field

A typical field for the off-spinner used to be leg-side biased (since that is the way the ball is turning). However, the trend now is for more fielders on the off-side – three in the ring, and two close. The short leg (a) is there for the inside-edge, or ball ricocheting off the glove. The silly point (b) for the possible bat-pad catch from a defensive prod to the off-break, and slip (c) for the 'arm ball' that is liable to take the edge if the batsman hasn't read it properly.

INTIMIDATING THE BATSMAN
The arrow shows the path of the off-spin. The men crouching in front of the bat (a) and (b) have both physical and psychological value.

KEY	
a short leg	**c** slip
b silly point	

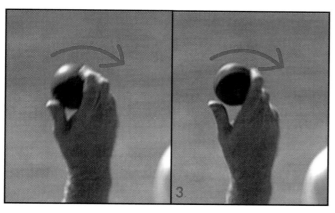

OFF-BREAK
Spin is imparted mainly with the first and second fingers. The thumb assists. The seam is then spinning from left to right but the condition of the pitch will determine how much turn is achieved.

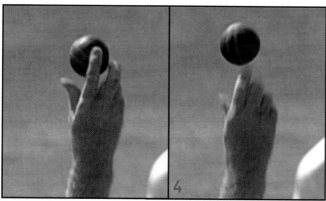

ARM BALL
This delivery starts with the same grip, but no spin is imparted and the ball is allowed to glide out of the hand, guided by the first finger only. It will bounce straight-on after pitching.

OFF-SPIN

The off-break

The release of the off-break and the arm ball look quite similar from the batsman's end, but up close they are subtly different. The off-break is spun with first and second fingers and wrist rotating to the right, the seam spinning at right-angles to the batsman (3). Ideally, it should land on the seam for extra purchase. The more spin imparted, the more the ball will 'dip' in flight, landing earlier than the batsman expects. A spinner who gets a lot of dip is described as having 'a good loop'. Sri Lanka's off-spinner Muralitharan imparts so much spin the ball dips alarmingly late in flight.

Arm ball

An off-break won't necessarily spin. If the pitch has a good grass covering or a glassy sheen, it will only deviate marginally. Only in very crumbly, or damp conditions, is it likely to 'turn square' as the spin grips the surface. By contrast, the arm ball never turns. Well, it's not supposed to. The ball is floated off the first finger, seam upright with no spin imparted (4). All being well, the batsman still thinks it's an off-break and will play for the turn. Instead, the ball goes straight, or if it's still got plenty of shine, might actually swing away a bit. For this reason, it's often called a 'drifter'.

The 'Mystery Ball'

So, the art of off-spin is being revived by two brilliant practitioners who have developed new techniques and subtle guiles. What makes Saqlain (and Muralitharan) so brilliant, is that he has developed a ball that, with an off-break action and release, actually spins the other way. He found that if he inverted the wrist in delivery, and bowled the ball out of the top of his hand rather than out of the front, it did occasionally break the opposite way.

This unique delivery, labelled his 'mystery ball' or 'wrong'un', has caused such trepidation among batsmen that they are rendered strokeless against Saqlain. It is such a delicate and subtle skill, batsmen have had real trouble identifying it. From behind, the mystery ball looks only marginally different to the ordinary off-break. But the front-on view (i.e. the batsman's view) shows how the mystery ball (6) is significantly different from the normal off-break (5). Basically, the mystery ball is bowled out of the back of the hand. Although his wrist is still moving in a left-to-right motion (i.e. for an off-break), this subtle variation imparts top-spin, and even a little leg-spin, on the ball. The final result is a ball spinning in the opposite direction to the way the batsman expects. If you look at the pictures below, the differences between the two deliveries are quite obvious. However, the bowler's hand is in this position for only a fraction of a second, and the difference isn't discernible to the batsman 22 yards' away. The mystery ball is wonderful to watch, unless you're the batsman.

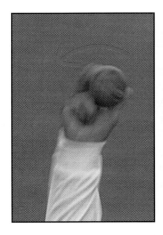

BATSMAN'S VIEW
The off break (5) and the mystery ball (6) as the batsman would see them. The wrist rotates in the same way for both balls. However, the off-break comes out of the front of the hand, whereas the mystery ball comes out of the back of the hand.

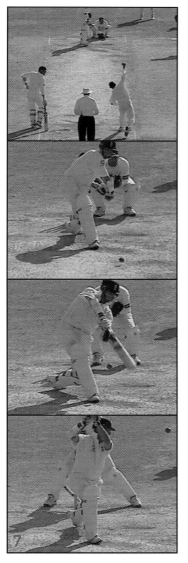

Entrapment

No other current off-spinner turns the ball both ways with the same action, and against Saqlain most batsmen are constantly guessing which way the ball will spin. Mostly they assume it's the normal off-break, turning from left to right. If it goes the other way, they're in danger of missing it by a mile. This is exactly how Marcus Trescothick was bamboozled (7). The ball landed in the rough outside the left-handers off stump, Trescothick, assuming it would spin away from him, went for a big drive. But it was the 'wrong 'un' and it darted 'through the gate' to bowl him. It was a brilliant piece of deception.

Using the crease

Usually, off-spinners bowl over the wicket to right-handers, and round the wicket to left-handers. The latter is particularly effective as the Test match wears on because there may be some rough to aim into. To confuse the left-hander further, the off-spinner can vary his angle with different positions on the crease. Robert Croft can take this to extremes, bowling from a bewildering range of places.

FULL OF MYSTERY
Trescothick is totally bamboozled by Saqlain's mystery ball, which spins through the gate.

CROFT'S CRAFT
Three deliveries from Robert Croft to the West Indies left-handers, each bowled from a different place on the crease.

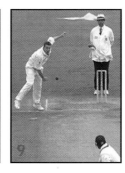

Left-arm Spin

Orthodox left-arm spin is considered more dangerous than off-spin as it spins away from the right-handed batsman (from right to left). Therefore, it can't be as easily 'kicked away' with the bat hidden behind the pad. Left-arm spinners are always striving for their 'magic' ball – pitching in line with the leg stump and turning to hit off stump – and their stock delivery constantly threatens the edge of the bat.

The two greatest post-war left-arm spinners in world cricket – Bishen Bedi (India) and Derek Underwood – were very different. Bedi got his wickets with flight and guile, while Underwood bowled flatter, with relentless accuracy. But their basic delivery was the same. Phil Edmonds and Phil Tufnell (11) have been the outstanding English left-arm spinners of the last two decades, though Ashley Giles looks as if he's starting to come into his own. The release of the left-arm spinner is a mirror image of the off break. The grip is with the first and second fingers (thumb underneath) and the wrist rotation is right to left.

GIVING IT A RIP
Phil Tufnell is here bowling orthodox left-arm spin, attempting to get a ball to pitch middle and hit off.

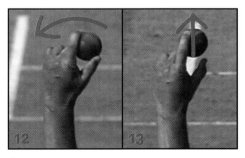

LEFT-ARM SPIN
Ashley Giles' left-arm spinner – turning from right to left (12) – and his arm ball, which 'drifts' the other way (13).

Compare these pictures of the New Zealander Daniel Vettori with the off-break (p.103) and you can see they're the same in reverse. Again, the seam is revolving roughly at right angles to the batsman, and the ball will turn more if it lands on the seam. A left-arm spinner's craft is all about slight variations of line, spin and speed while maintaining relentless accuracy. He too sometimes bowls an 'arm ball' (13), also the mirror image of the off-spinner's drifter, it is released seam up and floats in towards the batsman.

DANIEL VETTORI
A very strong body action, coiling and unravelling with the guiding hand unwinding from the left ear.

PHILIP TUFNELL
He doesn't spin the ball as much as Vettori because of less wind-up in his action, but he has excellent flight.

Body actions

As with any type of spin, some left-armers turn the ball more than others. This might be to do with the strength/size of their fingers and wrists, or it might be that one bowls 'rollers' (sort of floating out of his hand and not spinning much) and another gives it a real 'rip'. In the case of Vettori (a strong spinner of the ball) and Tufnell (more of a flight bowler) their differences have more to do with their body actions. Vettori really coils his body as he is preparing to deliver, before unwinding everything to release the ball (14). Tufnell's upper body doesn't coil as much, meaning he doesn't put as much 'work' on the ball (15), but he is extremely crafty.

ENTICEMENT
Here Phil Tufnell is bowling to Chris Cairns. Despite an energetic follow through, Tufnell varies his pace cleverly, often luring batsmen out of their crease with a classic ball-on-a-string delivery.

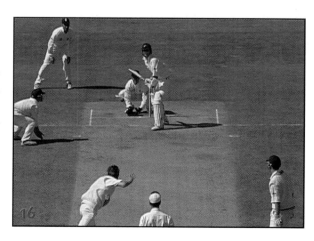

Left-arm Spinner's Field

Spinners probably use their field settings more strategically than quick bowlers. Good fielding is vital as the most common mode of dismissal against a spinner is caught. Their art is all about precision, and some slow bowlers are incredibly finnicky about their field, moving men half a yard and refusing to bowl until they are in exactly the right place. Middlesex and England left-arm spinner Phil Edmonds would always protest if he didn't get the field he wanted.

This is a good example of how a left-arm spinner is trying to lure a batsman to his doom (18). In many ways it's an orthodox left-armer's field. On the off-side there are three men saving one in the covers (just out of shot on the left), a slip (a) for the edge, and a silly point (b) for the bat-pad catch. The short extra cover (c) is there for the uppish drive, when the batsman doesn't quite get to the pitch.

What's more interesting is the leg-side field. The mid-on (d) you would expect, then there's a short fine leg

(e) which is there because the batsman facing (Hussain) is an avid sweeper and might get a top edge in that direction. The third leg-side man is out of the picture at deep square leg. There is no one at mid-wicket (see arrow), which appears an inviting gap. That's deliberate. This is a wearing Oval pitch and the ball is turning from right to left. The bowler (Vettori) is trying to tempt the batsman to angle the ball into that gap – against the spin – effectively making him play across the line and possibly get into trouble.

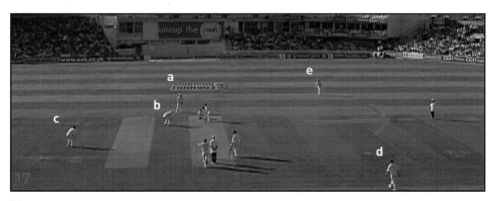

TEMPTING THE BATSMAN
A typical left-arm spinner's in-field on a turning pitch at The Oval. Note the large, tempting gap at mid-wicket (see arrow).

KEY	
a slip	**d** mid-on
b silly point	**e** short fine leg
c short extra cover	

What's it all About? – Chinaman

Very occasionally, you'll hear commentators going on about a chinaman. The origins of the name are obscure, but there might be an indirect connection with Shanghai. A chinaman is actually a ball from a normal left-arm spinner that turns the opposite way to his normal delivery (i.e. from left to right). Basically it's the mirror image of the right armer's leg break (see next page). There are two possible explanations for the term. Either it was coined after Ellis Achong, a West Indian of Chinese descent, who bowled this stuff for the West Indies in the 1930s. Or, more likely, it was a very un-PC reference to the perceived deviousness for which 'chinese' or 'chinamen' were known.

Chinaman googly

It's certainly a hard ball to play, and even harder to bowl, which explains why chinaman bowlers are rare. You'll see the odd one on the Indian sub-continent, but the only regular sighting in Test cricket is when either Australia's Michael Bevan or South Africa's Paul Adams is whistled up for a bowl. Just to complicate things even further, they can bowl the chinaman-googly, out of the back of the hand, which spins the opposite way to the chinaman and the same way as orthodox left-arm spin.

Other variations

You do get these quirky spin bowlers occasionally. One was Australia's John Gleeson, who bowled both off-breaks and leg breaks, apparently squeezing the ball out off a bent middle-finger. Another was the Indian Bhagwat Chandrasekhar, universally nicknamed 'Chandra' who snaked in off a ten-pace run to bowl lightening fast googlies, top spinners and occasional leg breaks with a withered arm. Few batsmen could read him and his ability to bowl the unplayable delivery still gives leading adversaries of the time, like Geoff Boycott and the Chappell brothers, sleepless nights.

Double joints

Sri Lanka's Matthiah Muralitharan continues to mesmerise modern batsmen. With a double-jointed wrist and a bowling arm he can't completely straighten, his action has often been questioned, but there's no doubt about the prodigious spin he extracts from any pitch. He can make the ball turn literally at right angles. He took 16 of England's 20 wickets to fall at The Oval in 1998 and, at the rate he is going, could end up taking more Test wickets than anyone in history.

Leg Spin and Googly

Leg spin is by far the most exciting and potentially devastating type of spin, and also the hardest to master. It is frequently described as 'wrist spin' while off-spin and left-arm spin are labelled as 'finger spin'. It seems a fairly subtle distinction since all three types use both wrist and fingers to turn the ball, but there we are.

Leg spin

Leg spin is a bit of a throwback to the early part of the twentieth century when leg spinners were almost ten a penny. The legendary Tich Freeman, only 5ft 2in, had an extraordinary first class career for Kent and England during which he took 3,776 wickets – the second most in cricket history. Not only will this now never be beaten, but it also suggests that English batsmen were as bad at playing leg spin in the 1920s as they are renowned to be today.

A new master

Leg spin was in the doldrums in world cricket until Shane Warne came on the scene in 1990 with his beach-boy image, vicious leg spin and exceptional accuracy. He found the going tough at first, taking 1-150 on his Test debut, but it wasn't long before he routed the all powerful West Indies and then England in 1993. His hard spun leg breaks and other devilish deliveries made him an Aussie hero and soon every young Australian wanted to be a 'leggie'.

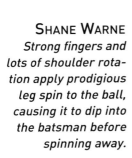

SHANE WARNE
Strong fingers and lots of shoulder rotation apply prodigious leg spin to the ball, causing it to dip into the batsman before spinning away.

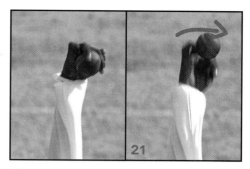

LEG BREAK
The ball spins out of the side of the hand and turns from right to left. This is the West Indian Nagamootoo.

GOOGLY
The same wrist rotation as the leg break, but the ball is released from the back of the hand, so it spins the other way.

What makes Warne's brand of leg spin so devastating is the amount of spin his strong hands and explosive action put on the ball. As with any leg spinner, his stock ball spins from right to left (away from the right-hander) but, because of the humming spin, as the ball moves through the air it dips in towards the batsman. (22). It is this dip, as much as the actual turn, that makes life so difficult for the batsman. The ball appears to veer in towards the pads, dropping down late in flight, before biting the pitch and spinning away. Warne, like all spinners, is classified as a 'slow' bowler, but his average ball is

around 56mph and so – at this speed, and with all that's happening on the ball – there is not much time to react.

The googly

A leg spinner's unique asset is the googly, if he can bowl it (not all can). This is the most misunderstood delivery in cricket. It's not nearly as difficult to comprehend as it is to play. The googly spins the opposite way from the leg break, i.e. from left to right (like an off-break). The clever thing is it's bowled with the same wrist action as the leg spinner, but the release out of the back of hand makes it spin the other way.

CONFIDENCE TRICKSTER
Warne has about five different deliveries including the 'Zooter', which drifts in without turning. Seeing a novice face him is like watching a newborn foal on roller skates.

Toppers and Flippers

A top-class leg spinner has two other deliveries in his armoury: a topper and a flipper. The top spinner has a release mid-way between the leggie and the googly. It goes straight on, dips in flight and usually kicks up from the pitch, like a top spin return in tennis. Because of its extra bounce it often hits the batsman on the glove or gets a top edge (23).

The flipper

The flipper is a fiendishly difficult delivery to bowl. Richie Benaud said it took him four years before he had the confidence to use it in a match.

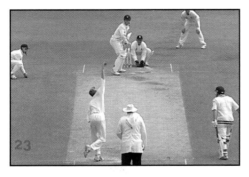

TOP SPINNER
Delivered out of the back of the hand, it goes straight on and bounces up.

FLIPPER
This delivery, sometimes called a back spinner, is released from the front of the hand, goes straight on and keeps low.

It's actually a back-spinner, bowled underhand in a motion a bit like clicking your fingers. It floats through the air in smiling innocence, then skids wickedly along the ground on landing, like a chopped backhand in tennis. Often it's bowled short, and the unsuspecting batsman lays back to cut, thinking the ball is a long hop. But when it bounces, it scuttles, pinning him on the ankle or sneaking under the bat and rattling into the base of the stumps (24).

Setting a field

With all these variations and contortions, leg spinners, it won't surprise you to know, are notoriously inaccurate. They are difficult to set a field for because of all the different spins and the possibility that they'll send down one ball every over asking to be spanked to the boundary. However, they are invaluable in that they can make something happen on any pitch and soon demand the kind of attacking field not seen for any other kind of spinner, with four men (slip, gully, silly point and short leg) clustered round the bat. On those days, they can bowl anyone out (as Mike Gatting remembers having received the 'Ball of the Century' from Warne in 1993). On other days, they can be an expensive luxury.

Spin Bowlers with most Test Wickets

No surprise to see Shane Warne heads this list, as he has singularly brought spin bowling back to the fore, and over the last ten years, terrorised and tormented every international batting order except India's. Muralitharan's performance is exceptional given that he is not yet 30 years old, has had the legality of his action questioned and has had little or no support from any bowlers at the other end.

Apart from Lance Gibbs, the others are all leg spinners or left-armers, but of varying styles. Bishen Bedi's loopy, drifty spin contrasted starkly with Derek Underwood's flatter, more relentless approach, and the leg spin of Benaud, Qadir and Chandrasekar couldn't be more different. Benaud was the master of cunning, Qadir a sorcerer in whites and Chandra's frail body still produced the fastest googlies ever known.

Greatest Spin Bowlers	
S K Warne (Aus)	366
L R Gibbs (WI)	309
M Muralitharan (SL)	303
D L Underwood (E)	297
A Kumble (India)	276
B S Bedi (India)	266
R Benaud (Aus)	248
B S Chandrasekar (Ind)	242
Abdul Qadir (Pakistan)	236
C V Grimmett (Aus)	216

Richie Benaud on the Art of Leg-spin Bowling

Here, Richie Benaud shares his insights into the art of leg-spin bowling. Nobody understands the skills and techniques of leg spin better – he took 266 Test wickets with leg spin and has analysed the actions of all subsequent exponents.

For over-the-wrist spin, grip the ball so that the seam runs across the first joint of the index finger and the first joint of the third finger. For the leg-break, and the overspinner or topspinner, the ball is spun off the third finger. The wrist is cocked, but definitely not stiffly cocked which would prevent flexibility. In delivering the ball, you look at the spot on the pitch on which you wish the ball to land, your bowling hand starts level with your face and then describes what could loosely be termed an anti-clockwise circle to the point of delivery.

The position of the bowling hand dictates in which direction the ball will spin. At the moment of delivery, the positioning of the hand is as follows:

Leg-break

In delivery, the back of the hand is facing the face. (The ball will spin out with the seam rotating in an anti-clockwise direction towards slip.)

Overspinner or topspinner

In delivery, the back of the hand is facing the sky and then the bats-

man. (The ball will spin out with the seam rotating in an anti-clockwise direction and towards the batsman.)

Wrong'un

In delivery, the back of the hand is first facing the sky and then the ground. (The ball will spin out with the seam rotating in an anti-clockwise direction towards fine-leg.)

You should practise the hard-spun leg-break 90% of the time, the variations only 10%. You should be side-on to the batsman and looking over your front shoulder as you deliver the ball and then your bowling hand will finish up going past your front thigh. This means, if you have done it correctly, your body will have pivoted and rotated anti-clockwise. This 'pivot' is of great importance. If you bowl a ball that is too short, you can be almost certain it happened because your body was 'chest-on' to the batsman, rather than side-on, and you dragged the ball down into the pitch. When you are bowling in a net, make a white shoe cleaner mark the size of a 20 cent piece, on what seems to you to be a good length – that is, with the leg-break pitching where you would not like it to land if you were batting.

Never have your bowling arm at or past the perpendicular when you deliver the ball; it should be at least a few inches lower than the perpendicular.

Don't even think about learning the 'flipper' before you have mastered the leg-break, topspinner and wrong'un.

Keep it simple

Attend to the basics first (focusing on the five points listed below); if you can't do that, then the more complicated things will be impossible anyway. It is possible to extend some of those points but the one thing of which you can be guaranteed is that common sense will always outweigh rhetoric and complication.

1. **Patience:** bowling is a tough game and you will need to work on a batsman with your stock ball, sometimes for several overs, before putting your plan into action. It may not work the first time or even the second. (If you take a wicket on average every 10 overs in Test cricket, you will have a better strike-rate than any of O'Reilly, Grimmett, or Warne. If you take a wicket on average every eight overs, you could have the best strike-rate of any modern-day Test bowler, fast or slow.)

2. **Concentration:** anything less than 100% concentration running into bowl is unpardonable. The spot on the pitch where you want the ball to land should be the most important thing in your mind from the moment you turn at your bowling mark. (If someone offered you $10,000 if you could throw a ball and hit an object 19 yards away, in trying to win the money would you, as you were throwing, look at someone standing nearby, or at some other object?)

3. **Economy:** this game is a war between you and the batsmen. (Is there some very good reason you want to allow him more than two runs an over, thus possibly giving your captain the idea you should be taken off?)

4. **Attitude:** calm, purposeful aggression and a clear mind are needed, plus a steely resolve that no batsman will get the better of you over a long period of time. Always remember as well that cricket is a game to be enjoyed and that you are responsible at all times for ensuring that play is conducted within the spirit of the game, as well as within the Laws. (In other walks of life, you will want to be mentally strong and on top of the opposition. Is there some particular reason why, within the spirit of the game, this should not be the case in your battle with the batsmen?)

6. **Practice:** all practice should be undertaken with a purpose. (You think hard before doing most other things, why should you allow cricket practice to be dull and boring?)

Bowling into the Rough

You hear a lot of talk about it being important to have a spinner in a Test team, in the likely event of fielding last in the match. By the fourth innings, the pitch could be really damaged and pockmarked, and here the spinner can come into his own. In particular, there will be a lot of footmarks left by the bowlers down both sides of the pitch. It can be quite pitted in places. The ball bouncing in these areas can do almost anything, which is why the spinner aims into them. A spinner bowling into the rough is partly what makes chasing anything above 150 on the fifth day of a Test a bit of a lottery.

Unpredictability

The worst rough will usually be outside the right-handers leg stump, because the majority of quick bowlers are right-arm and operate over the wicket. The rough constitutes quite a large area on this fifth day Pakistani pitch (25). Both teams' spinners aimed into it and the ball behaved unpredictably, sometimes jumping, sometimes spinning viciously, sometimes scuttling. This makes the batsmen apprehensive about playing normal shots, the runs gradually dry up, until they become desperate and attempt something rash.

25

'Bowling into the rough makes chasing 150 to win very difficult'

TAKING CARE
This ball looks like a free hit for the batsman but there is a lot of rough. As the ball hits the rough area it can behave unpredictably and the batsman has to be careful.

OUT OF THE PARK
A well directed ball into the rough by Ian Salisbury is met by an even better directed hit from Inzamam ul Haq.

BACK IN THE HUTCH
This ball, into the rough, from Ashley Giles jumped up and hit the batsman on the glove, giving Stewart a simple catch.

Cricket or football?

It was interesting to see the different ways that Pakistan and England approached playing this type of bowling. Whereas the English batsmen tended to 'kick' most of these deliveries away, hiding the bat behind their pad (the ball is pitching outside leg stump so lbw's are ruled out), the Pakistanis were intent on scoring off most of them. Sometimes it worked and sometimes it didn't. Inzamam ul Haq, a vast man with an even vaster weight of stroke, sized up this ball into the rough from Ian Salisbury, and larruped it ten rows back into the terraces (26). His younger and less powerful colleague Salim Elahi had visions of doing something similar against Ashley Giles. However, the ball landed in the rough, leapt onto his glove and was acrobatically caught by Alec Stewart. Elahi's innings was over (27).

A test of patience

Left-handed batsmen dread the rough a great deal more than right-handers because they can't just kick the ball away. They're forced to play at a lot of balls that are liable to misbehave. This doesn't necessarily mean they're going to get out more, though. It just means they need to be extra watchful (or extra lucky). That, in fact, is a microcosm of the spinner's art. On average, they need twice as many overs to take their wickets as pace bowlers do. They're winkling batsmen out rather than torpedoing them. In the duel between the batsman and the spinner, it's a test of patience more than anything else; as Warne himself once said, 'bowl a few maidens and the wickets will follow.' While the modern spinner might release the ball fairly slowly, he nevertheless thinks and acts as aggressively as the pacemen.

FIELDING

There is no escaping the fact that fielding occupies most of the hours any cricketer spends out in the middle. The old school may regularly debate whether Test-match batting standards have deteriorated in the last twenty years and bemoan modern boorish bowling, but one thing brooks no argument: the standard of fielding has improved out of all recognition. The fitness and agility of teams like Australia, South Africa and, more recently, England is outstanding.

A Question of Attitude

Test cricket has benefited enormously from the improvements in fielding brought about by the increasing popularity of one-day cricket. But really it is an attitude thing – fielders are now proud to show off their accurate throws or sliding stops. The top teams acknowledge the value of exceptional fielding, in all forms of the game, and focus a lot of attention on it. There was a good deal of evidence on England's recent tour of Pakistan, however, to suggest that some Test teams still lag behind.

Alert, athletic fielding and sharp catching can transform an ordinary bowling attack into a useful one, and turn a good attack into a great one. Batsmen surrounded by predatory fielders feel hemmed in, gasping for air. Frequently they suffocate. Diving stops and brilliant catches invigorate the fielding side, fumbles and drops demoralise them. Slick operators like Jonty Rhodes and Ricky Ponting are like extra bowlers – they take wickets not only through catches and run outs but also by the indecision and paralysis they inflict on batsmen.

It's not as if you can pick on weak fielders in a Test side these days either. Gone are the days when you could always take one run to the lumbering batsman at mid-on, or guarantee the hefty quick bowler would amble round the boundary and fail to stop the ball with an out-stretched boot. Now everyone's expected to dive, chase, or pirouette and throw the ball in flat. And the game's all the better for it. Test teams will have specialist fielders – that has always been the case in the slips, but now the whole team will have been coached and drilled to maximise their effectiveness. Throwing, catching, sliding stops and backing-up are a key part of team preparations. It is when things are going well in the field that a team really comes together.

INVIGORATION
A difficult half chance is snatched out of the air. The fielding team will all join in the celebrations and, for the next few overs, everyone will be fired up.

Slip Fielding

Few overs are bowled in a Test match without at least one man in the slips. This is not just to keep the wicket-keeper company, though on batsmen-friendly pitches it might look like it. Slip is probably the most important fielding position in the game. Without one, a batsman will feel much more at liberty to have a go at good balls outside the off stump, knowing, if he gets a thickish edge, there's no one there to catch it.

Sod's law dictates that you can stand at slip, concentrating furiously for hours, and not touch the ball once, then, when you've given up hope of ever getting any action and are contemplating where to go out for dinner, a chance comes along and you shell it. Slip fielding needs great powers of concentration, never mind quick reflexes. It's a case of switching off most of the time, and just switching on for those crucial four seconds when the ball is 'live'. It's why opening batsmen usually make good 'slippers' and bowlers are bad ones – their concentration is going to be seriously impaired if they're fuming about a lucky edge in their last over. It also helps if you have big hands – Graeme Hick's are like buckets (3).

Proportionately more chances go to second slip than first (the keeper often poaches ones going to first) so the best 'copper' (catcher) always stands there. Because of the different angles involved, specialist first slips rarely stand at second, and vice-versa.

FIRST SLIP
The ball comes at a nice height for Brian Lara to take this slip catch. He was lucky that, on this occasion, the keeper wasn't tempted to go for it.

BUCKET HANDS
Graeme Hick is an excellent slip fielder who has taken hundreds of catches. It helps to have hands much larger than average (mine in the foreground).

Standing styles

Standing styles vary. Atherton and Hick, part of England's regular slip cordon, prefer the slightly more crouched stance (4), Hick even resting his hands on his knees, which most coaching manuals advise against. In reality, it's whatever feels comfortable and Hick has snaffled hundreds of catches – some of them blinders.

Normally, an opening bowler will start with three slips, more is unusual. Here there are four, and two gullies (5).

COMFORT IS VITAL
You may be standing in the slips for hours – Atherton (right) prefers to crouch, Hick is more upright.

STANDING APART
Slip cordons are staggered. The first slip (circled), standing behind the wicket-keeper, is a long way back.

There's a simple explanation – the West Indies were 23-4 and the wicket was a minefield. The slips take their positions from the keeper. First slip will stand a little deeper (fine edges carry further), second slip on roughly the same line, third slip a little closer.

In Australia, where the bounce is consistently higher, slip fielders adopt a more upright stance. This shot from the 1970s is interesting not only because of the two slip fielders' stances (6), but also because of the extraordinary wind-up in Jeff Thomson's action. The crouched figure batting is Graham Gooch, on his Test debut.

STANDING UP
Australian slip catchers stand more upright because, on their pitch, the ball will bounce higher.

Where Slip Fielders Stand

Slip fielders can stand as close as they dare to the bat, but they better not stand too close together or they'll get in each other's way. Daily practice will determine who goes for what in the slip cordon when the ball flies between two of them (it is a bit like playing doubles in tennis), but sometimes instinct takes over. In the sequence below Graeme Hick does very well not to be put off by Graham Thorpe's outstretched hand and still take the catch (7).

You can't fault Thorpe's enthusiasm, but he probably shouldn't have gone for it. It was closer to Hick and therefore his catch. Not only have there been cases of dropped catches but also broken fingers when one slip fielder gets in the way of another.

Gully

Gully fieldsman, (so called because they are in the 'gully' or gap between slips and cover) will tend to vary where they stand according to the pitch and the batsman. For a slow pitch, or a nervous, prodding batsman, they'll need to be up close. They will creep up as near as they dare, hoping for something to pop up off the bat handle. On faster pitches, or to cater for batsman inclined to have a serious waft at anything outside off stump, it is wise to retreat a bit.

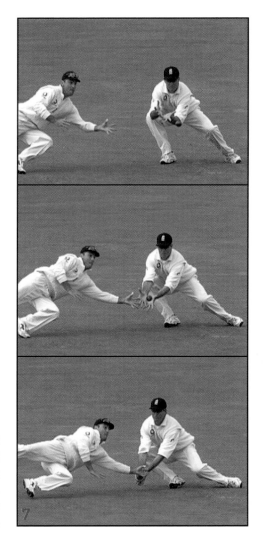

KNOW YOUR PLACE
To be a good slip, or any kind of close fielder, you need the quickest reactions, but here instinct nearly causes a mix up.

Short Leg and Silly Point

Boot hill, bat pad, short leg – call it what you like, but you'll usually find the junior pro in residence there, crouching under the helmet staring at the batsman's backside. It sounds harsh, but a stint at short leg is part of a young player's initiation into Test cricket. You are supposed to be there to snaffle catches that pop up off the glove or the inside edge, but you won't be surprised to hear it's not great fun. You're either grubbing around in the dust at the batsman's feet, or you're a standing target for a brutal swipe on the leg side.

SHORT LEG
Directly in the line of fire on the leg side, this fielder has paid the price (8).

SILLY POINT
Less mortally dangerous but with a good chance of a blow to the shins (9).

A short leg will don box, helmet, shin guards and anything else that might soften the blow of leather on bone. However, it's still a precarious business; particularly, bearing in mind batsmen will do their best to try to shift a short leg by playing aggressive shots in their direction (8). There is no record of anyone being killed at short leg, but that's little compensation if you've just felt the wind of an expansive sweep as it flies past your left ear.

Silly point

Silly point, on the other side of the wicket, is slightly safer (generally the ball isn't hit in the air through this area) but you can still get serious shin bruising. Silly points are also looking for little bat-pad catches as the batsman pushes forward (usually to spinners). With 'pad play' more and more in vogue, the silly point is kept interested. Often they stand very close, as much to get in the batsman's eyeline as to be able to pluck the ball from virtually under the batsman's nose.

SIGHT LINE
A bat-pad fielder mustn't encroach on to the cut area of the pitch but he can get in the batsman's eyeline.

Cover Point

Usually, a team's sprightliest fielder is stationed at cover point. South Africa's Jonty Rhodes has made this position his own, as has Ricky Ponting of Australia. Derek Randall was a legend there for England, as were Clive Lloyd and Viv Richards for the West Indies. It's a vital position as most defensive shots go in this direction, and you can expect batsmen to look for quick singles in that area. Both Rhodes and Ponting take regular 'wickets' with direct hits on the stumps.

COVER POINT
Cover point is square of the wicket, about 25 yards from the bat. His main task is to prevent the single.

Cover point is not the easiest place to field as the ball will be bouncing and skidding across old wicket ends and bowler's footholds from previous matches. Originally, this position was so close it was practically on the 'point' of the bat, hence its name, now it has retreated some 25 yards. Not only is he there to stop the batsman taking easy singles with little defensive pushes, but also to get in the way of cuts and square drives. Rhodes, in particular, charges in from quite a deep starting point and throws himself around like an athletic goalkeeper.

The young Pakistani Imran Nazir is the Jonty Rhodes of the sub-continent, which is quite a development since Pakistan is not famous for producing brilliant fielders. His prowess can be seen well in the incident below: a breathtaking catch from a Marcus Trescothick uppish cut (12).

PREDATORY INSTINCT
Imran Nazir is in a great balanced position as the batsman hits the ball, ready to spring in either direction. His instinctive soar and grasp of a firmly hit shot almost defies belief.

Fielding 'In the Ring'

Any man fielding 'in the ring' – i.e. the positions about 25 yards from the bat, which are there to stop the batsmen taking easy singles – is expected to attack the ball. It helps if you're walking in and on your toes as the bowler bowls, something you're taught in the under-elevens but occasionally forget.

As soon as they come in, batsmen will scrutinise fielders 'in the ring', assessing which ones are quick, which ones are slower, and which hand they throw with. They will earmark tired-looking (or clumsy-moving) bowlers as targets for quick singles, and they will also note the left-handed fielders. Numerous batsmen have been run out having knocked the ball to what they thought was the man's wrong side, then seeing him pick up the ball left-handed and hurl down the stumps before they've barely got halfway. For spinners, nimble fielders are often posted in places where you would least expect them – short fine leg for instance – trying to inhibit batsmen from playing their favourite shots.

Graham Thorpe, in the focal position of backward point, gets into good shape here to pounce on the ball and throw as the batsmen attempt to pinch a single (13). He was perhaps a little deep though and anyway the throw missed. Hitting the wicket from side-on with one stump to aim at is something the Australians excel at, but it doesn't come without endless practice. The most famous cover fielder of all, the legendary Colin Bland used to demonstrate his skills before play, with a dozen throws at a single stump from 25 yards. Apparently he rarely missed.

KEEP MOVING
Fielders 'in the ring' walk in as the bowler bowls so they are on their toes to stop quick singles and seize on run-out chances.

Boundary Fielders

Boundary fielders are usually the bowlers – less-agile movers dispatched to deeper pastures. It may be to allow them to recuperate after delivering a fiery over, or to let off steam if they've been collared. Or it may be to hide them, because their fielding really is a bit ropey.

Here, further from the bat, you've got a bit more time to see the ball before having to crank yourself into action, and you can have a quick swig from the water bottle the 12th man has left for you the other side of the rope. You're also close enough to the spectators to have a quick chat with one but this does have a downside. If your over has just been carted around the park (or you've misfielded) you will be confronted by chants of 'eeyore, eeyore' or other uncomplimentary observations.

Objective view

Fielding on the boundary does give you a more detached view of the game, from where you might notice a useful flaw in a batsman's technique.

Or it can be a reflective place where you dwell on the success of your last over and lap up the applause. This is what Courtney Walsh is doing here (14), enjoying the deception of his fifth ball – a slower delivery – that trapped Thorpe lbw for the second time in the series.

Bowlers have pretty good throwing arms as a rule, and even the tallest ones will put in a dive these days to stop the four, rather than the age-old tactic of sticking out a boot. It pays to be alert on the boundary too, since the odd dynamic bit of work can lift the team. Darren Gough's stunning full-length catch at third man to catch Sherwin Campbell at Lord's in 2000 turned the match and the series.

ENGLAND
254-7

LONG LEG
Courtney Walsh is made for this position and not just because he is 6ft 6in. Like many bowlers, he is an error-prone fielder, best kept a good distance from the bat.

The Slide Stop

The slide stop has really been in vogue the last ten years or so. The ex-Sussex and England (and briefly Durham) player Paul Parker started it all off, if I'm not much mistaken. He was a brilliant fielder who realised that by sliding up to the ball, even some way from the boundary, you could collect it and jump into a good throwing position all in one movement. He found this method faster than gathering the ball in mid-stride and regaining your balance to throw. Also, breaking your momentum to stoop and pick up the ball, turn and throw is more stressful on your knees.

As fielding has become more athletic, more and more players use the slide stop, not only near the boundary but also in quick dashes from the infield. Chris Scofield is one of England's best fielders and here uses the slide stop to restrict a likely boundary to only two runs (15). The old-fashioned method would be to flick the ball back, overrun the rope, then wheel round and return to pick up the ball. The batsmen would have coasted three for certain. Here, the process (from first picture to fourth) takes less than two seconds and the batsmen weren't even thinking about a third. The only downside, of course, is that it does severely mess up your whites.

TOTAL COMMITMENT
This is a sight not seen 20 years ago. Modern boundary fielding requires speed, agility, resilient knees and lots of spare whites.

Throwing

If you look into an average English secondary school playground, you will see that most kids have more of an aptitude for kicking a ball than for throwing it. If you do the same at an American school, you'll see the reverse. Throwing has always been a rather weak link in English cricket – there seem to be numerous players who have shoulder problems or have 'thrown their arms out' and few who can whizz an exocet into the keeper's gloves from 60 yards – Hick is one exception.

Perhaps for this reason, a baseball throwing coach, Julien Fountain has been employed by the English Cricket Board to help improve throwing technique at all levels. It's a good idea, since having someone with a really good arm effects long-distance run outs and incites all sorts of indecision in the running between the wickets. The Zimbabwean Heath Streak, for example, has run out countless batsmen whizzing in a flat throw from the cover boundary over the top of the stumps.

The Australians use their throwing prowess quite provocatively, zipping in stinging returns to the wicket-keeper from the in-field even when the batsmen haven't considered running. It's a kind of testy reminder that they're there and they're going to make the batsmen's lives as uncomfortable as possible. Their own wicket-keeper's hands must be in a bit of a state by the end, mind you, receiving all those missiles. But it serves a vital purpose, the batsman knows he's surrounded by predators.

PERFECT TECHNIQUE
This is England's best cover fielder, Nasser Hussain, about to let fly. He doesn't have a mega-powerful throw but it is deadly accurate.

Fielding Positions

The diagram below shows the basic fielding positions adopted for a right-handed batsman. There are, however, many further variations. The wicket-keeper (and accompanying slip), for example, may 'stand up' to the wicket for a spinner but move well back for a fast bowler. Ultimately, the captain is responsible for setting the field to the counter the strengths and exploit the weaknesses of each batsman. In practice, however, the bowlers will always have a major say.

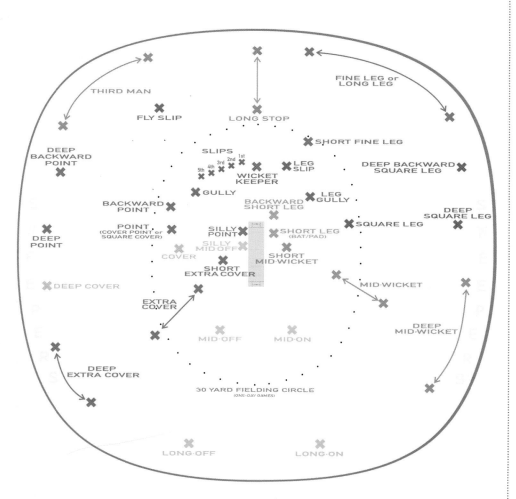

WICKET-KEEPING

Wicket-keepers are the new all-rounders. They are no longer selected simply for their keeping ability – their batting talent is of enormous importance. The keeper is the focal point of a team's fielding, and the vocal point – relied on throughout the day to urge on bowlers and fielders. They must, of course, be prepared to deal with every ball that's bowled in a day's play. His is a job that requires the ability to concentrate all day and stay 'up', able to keep things happening in the field.

The Focal Point

The wicket-keeper batsman is not a new phenomenon. Les Ames kept wicket and batted in the middle order for England in the 1930s, and Ferouk Enginner actually opened for India on occasions in the seventies. Keeping legends like Alan Knott and Rodney Marsh were also prolific run-getters. However, all these great glovemen were chosen on wicket-keeping merit. Now, the emphasis has changed. A keeper who can't make a significant contribution with the bat is almost immediately overlooked, regardless of his keeping pedigree.

Alec Stewart for instance is, by his own admission, an inferior keeper to Jack Russell (though he's still pretty good). But his batting prowess is a priceless asset, giving England far more options. With Stewart, England can, if they want, field five specialist bowlers and still have six proper batsmen. His all-round ability means they can build a team around him. A keeper less able with the bat can only be accommodated by omitting a bowler or a batsman. Bob Taylor, a brilliant keeper and limited batsman who played 57 Tests for England in the late 1970s, acknowledges he wouldn't get in the side now. This change of emphasis has been hastened by the domination of pace bowling. To pace bowling, keepers spend most of their time 'standing back' – an easier skill than grubbing around to spin 'standing-up' (to the stumps).

His key role in the field as the vocal centre means that the keeper needs to be a talker. This constant stream of comment and advice may seem to be almost automatic but it helps the bowler and fielders to stay focused. Taking all their responsibilities into account, and the fact that, after several long sessions in the field, they may be expected to soon strap the pads on and make some runs, they have probably the most onerous task in the modern game.

LEGENDS
Two wicket-keeping greats: Rodney Marsh keeping and Alan Knott batting. Both these keepers had huge presence both behind the stumps and wielding the willow.

Standing Back

Wicket-keepers are great individualists, each with their own distinguishing quirks. Alan Knott would be forever exercising during a long day, Rod Marsh incessantly chewing. Alec Stewart, a fastidious man, brushes imaginary dust off his gloves and fiddles with his collar after every ball. Their gloves are incredibly precious items, which they constantly, almost lovingly, reface and repair. Jack Russell used to keep his under his pillow at night.

JACK RUSSELL
Russell stands at an angle to the wicket – facing the way he's likely to move.

ALEC STEWART
Stewart also stands at an angle – this is mainly a British keeping trait.

Keeping styles vary enormously, but among English keepers it's in vogue to stand back with your body positioned slightly at an angle to the pitch. As disciples of Knott, both Russell (2) and Stewart (3) do it, the reason being the bowlers are mainly probing for outside edges. Therefore, the majority of their takes will be beside, or in front of, the slips so they may as well be half-going in that direction. Most international keepers regard this as eccentric, and squat facing straight down the pitch.

STANDING BACK
How far the keeper (arrowed) stands back dictates where the slip fielders stand. First slip is a bit deeper.

How far the keeper decides to stand back is always a talking point. Some prefer to take the ball below the waist, others chest high. Where the keeper stands is vital to the team, as the slip fielders take their positions from it (4). First slip will normally be two yards deeper than the keeper, second slip about on the same line, and the rest staggered in an arc from there. Stewart here is a long way back because Andy Caddick is getting a lot of lift from the pitch (8). If you see edges not carrying to slips and the keeper taking the ball round his ankles, they are all standing too deep.

Right height

The perfect height to take the ball is about where Jack Russell accepts this one (5). He is a very fidgety keeper, always on the move (and a very noisy one too). But, at the critical moment, he's always in the right position. He's as famous for the appalling state of his kit as he is for his brilliant catching, but there is method in his tattiness. He stitches and patches his precious gloves every day (note the tape round the base of each finger) and sticks bits of material on his sun hat so that it's heavy and won't blow off. This hat has been with him on the field for all but a handful of his 500 first-class games, and once caught fire when he tried to dry it in an oven. His pads – the modern light-

THE LIVED-IN LOOK
Everything about Jack Russell's keeping is perfect except the state of his kit. The gloves and hat have travelled the world.

weight keeping version – are quite a contrast to the cumbersome old-style ones Rod Marsh is wearing on p.130.

Dealing with uneven bounce

Keepers dread pitches with uneven bounce, especially ones that keep low. They can't afford to stand too close with bowlers letting fly at 90mph, and so have to be prepared to take the odd ball on the second bounce. Because the ground immediately behind the wicket is not always completely flat, they risk taking the odd one on the body. Stewart is facing just such a risk here (6) – the ball dying off the pitch and bouncing a yard in front of him. There's a real danger of it kicking up into his face, but he does well to keep his eye on it and ultimately take it cleanly. Tidying up irregularities like this is the mark of a top class keeper, and gives the fielders extra confidence in the same way a brilliant goalkeeper reassures a team.

WEARING PITCHES
As a pitch gets more worn, the ball tends to 'die' after bouncing, forcing keepers to take it on the half volley.

Standing Up

Crouching behind the stumps to spinners is known as 'standing up'. Because you're standing up (to the stumps), there is less time to react and the ball might occasionally jump and turn. Added to that, the batsman's body often obscures the keeper's view and the bat may be swishing inches away from his nose.

The keeper needs to be able to move sharply, have good reflexes and precise handiwork. The only benefit in 'standing up' is that he hasn't got to run in to the wicket every ball to take a fielder's throw.

Bowlers who turn the ball away from the bat are generally easier to keep to, since the keeper always has a clear view of the ball. A ball spinning into the batsman can be obscured by bat, leg or body and sometimes miss everything. This is clearly exhibited by Stewart, keeping here (for Surrey) to the bowling of Saqlain Mushtaq (7). The ball is the orthodox off-break and, if pitched straight, it disappears from the keepers view as it turns down the leg-side. It's a combination of skill and luck if he takes it cleanly.

BLOCKED VIEW
A ball turning into the batsman and veering down the leg side is difficult to take because the batsman obscures it.

Below is Saqlain's mystery ball (8), which turns away from the batsman. It pitches on an identical line, but, as it's spinning past the outside edge, Stewart can see it all the way.

CLEAR SIGHT
A ball turning away from the right-hander is easier to collect because the keeper has full view of it. Here, the

unlucky batsman conveniently overbalances after missing the ball and is comprehensively stumped.

WAIT FOR IT

This is the same stumping incident as (8), but from side-on. You can see that Alec Stewart doesn't grab at the ball, he waits for it to arrive (taking a ball in front of the stumps is not allowed) and the batsman to leave his ground before whipping off the bails. It's split second action.

Good Handiwork

A keeper is not allowed to take the ball in front of the stumps. If he does, it's a no ball. It must be tempting sometimes, when the wicket-keeper senses that the batsman is about to miss one, to try to grab it early. Stewart resists that temptation in this stumping (8) and (9) waiting until the ball has passed the stumps, and the batsman has overbalanced, before collecting the ball and whipping off the bails. A batsman who just has a foot or bat on the line when the bails are removed, incidentally, is out. He must have some part of body or bat grounded behind the line to be safe. What keepers probably dislike most of all is standing up to bowlers aiming into the rough outside leg stump. The ball can do anything from here, as we've seen: bounce, scuttle, spin or go straight on. They have hardly any view of the ball, especially with a huge man like Inzamam ul Haq batting (10) and may also have to peer through a dust cloud stirred up by a swirling bat. Keeping in these situations is an absolute lottery, and since they don't get danger money, some have started wearing gum shields and even helmets when confronted with it. A few unblemished hours of this and they've certainly earned their 'keep'.

TOTAL ECLIPSE

The keeper's biggest nightmare: trying to take balls bouncing into the rough, while hefty batsmen take muscular swings.

CAPTAINCY

Captaincy in cricket is more important than leadership in any other sport. In the same way that an orchestra cannot perform without its conductor, the cricket team won't function without its captain. The main reason for this is cricket takes so long that the players' intensity cannot be sustained without some kind of direction. Excitement and adrenaline alone don't motivate the team as they do in short games like football or rugby. Also, because a Test match can take five days, conditions and situations can change dramatically, demanding new responses.

Selection

Historically, most captains were batsmen. It was a class thing; batsmen were 'gentlemen'. It's still predominantly true today, batsmen generally make good captains. In the last twenty-five years all the best Test captains – Mike Brearley, Mark Taylor, Steve Waugh, etc – have all been top-order batsmen. (Nasser Hussain is now staking his claim to be included in this top bracket.) Before the current era, two of the best post-war captains were allrounders: Richie Benaud and Ray Illingworth. They appreciated both aspects of the game but didn't have the burden of top-order batting or opening the bowling.

A Test captain's list of duties does not extend to paying for tea and phoning in the score to the local paper, as it does in club cricket. It's an extremely complex and involved job nonetheless. His responsibilities can be divided into six areas:

1. Selection
2. The Toss
3. Motivation
4. Tactics
5. Declarations and follow-ons
6. Media

The first task

A captain's influence on selection varies. The tradition in Australia is for a selection committee to meet, then hand the chosen eleven over to the captain. Occasionally, in the past, they would select the best eleven players first, then pick the captain from them. However, they didn't have much success with that method.

In England, a captain is usually nominated for a term (either a tour or a series). He has full involvement in selection. Mike Brearley said he would have hated to have been

> '**Captaincy is 90 percent luck and 10 percent talent. But don't try it without that 10 percent**'
>
> RICHIE BENAUD

handed a team he had had no part in choosing, because he was the one who had to walk onto the field with them. The current vogue is for the captain to be one of three or four voices in the selection committee, but he may have the final say if a decision is split.

Selection is one of the captain's biggest headaches. In any team there will always be someone not pulling his weight, but when do you replace him, and who with? Much of the debate will centre round the balance of the side. How many front-line bowlers do we need on this pitch, against these batsmen? Do we need one spinner, two, or none at all? Only at the end of play will he know if he had the right team on the day.

The Toss

The captain announces his final eleven to his opposite number at the toss, which takes place half an hour before the start of play. Except in extraordinary circumstances, the make up of the team can't be changed after this point. The home captain will spin the coin and the visiting captain will call. Contrary to popular belief, even if the coin has come down heads in all the previous five Tests of a series, there is still a 50-50 chance it will come down heads again.

To bat or not to bat?

One of England's most distinguished captains, Colin Cowdrey, had firm beliefs about what to do if you won the toss. 'Nine times out of ten,' he'd say, 'you should automatically bat first. The other time you should think about fielding, but then bat anyway.' It worked for him (England lost only two of the nine series during his tenure as captain), but things are a little more sophisticated now. If there's any perceived dampness under the surface, most teams will elect to bowl first, either in a positive move, expecting their bowlers to make good use of the conditions, or as a negative one, not wanting to expose their batsmen to such a bowler-friendly situation. 'Sticking 'em in' is a far more accepted course of action than it used to be.

Occasionally, a captain will do the unexpected. At Old Trafford in 1997, Mark Taylor won the toss on an obviously damp pitch and elected to bat. This wasn't as foolhardy as it sounded. His batsmen dexterously negotiated the early movement, and the large, deep footmarks left by the England bowlers on the tacky surface, created perfect rough areas around the right-handers' leg stump, which Shane Warne exploited brilliantly later in the game.

The captain who wins the toss is supposed to tell his opposite number immediately what he has decided to do. He will also make a quick sign to the dressing room, either wielding an imaginary bat or swinging his arm in a bowling motion, to indicate what the team need to be ready for. The decision will usually be a consensus – he'll have canvassed opinion from colleagues, selectors, ground staff, quite probably old players and commentators found wandering about on the middle, and perhaps even a weather expert.

Sometimes the variety of suggestions is more confusing than it is helpful. Against Zimbabwe in 2000, Nasser Hussain had heard so many conflicting opinions, he didn't know what to do two minutes before the flick of the coin. Having won the toss, he followed his hunches and chose to bowl. It was a good decision. Within six overs Zimbabwe were 8-3 and soon after lunch were bundled out for 83.

Motivation

You get all types of captains. Loud, hands-on-hips types (Mike Gatting); quiet, detached types (Mike Atherton); disciplinarians (Alec Stewart); *laissez-faire*-ists (David Gower); fitness fanatics (Graham Gooch). The best captains employ a range of responses – emotional in some situations, philosophical in others, and know when to be stern and when to be sympathetic. Sometimes the whip is required, on other occasions the carrot is more appropriate. Mike Brearley, England's most successful captain, described the job as 'a bit like gardening – some plants need fertilizer to thrive, others need pruning'. A coaxing word for one and a cattle prod for another.

Communication

Having said that, a general outline of tactics is necessary in the dressing room – a pep talk before each session of play. This may be imparted in measured tones, as in 'It'd be nice to get three out before lunch' or 'Now let's not forget that Smith is very strong against anything short', or in more forceful ones: 'I told you Smith [80 not out] was a good hooker and puller. Anyone listening out there?'

Fred Trueman and his ilk would be quick to say that any Test cricketer worth his salt shouldn't need telling how to do his job, or require any motivation. 'Three lions on my chest were good enough for me,' etc. But players do need direction and, with the endless amount of international cricket played these days, the odd gee up. Nasser Hussain addresses his players in a little huddle on the field, just before heading out to the middle, as a final reminder of what's at stake.

Once play is underway, the captain's motivating words are on a more individual basis. He might sense a bowler is just going through the motions and chivvy him into greater effort, or take him off and let him stew on the boundary for a while until he's champing at the bit. He might be aware of someone feeling a bit of a spare part and give him an earlier bowl than he might have expected. He also has to be strong enough to take that bowler off again if he doesn't deliver.

Canvassing opinion from other members of the team, however junior, is also a good way of ensuring everyone feels important. Asking others what it would be best to do next is good team psychology and it doesn't mean you have to follow their suggestion. Mike Brearley suggests, in his classic book *The Art of Captaincy*, that charisma is not a prerequisite for a captain, but communication is. However icy the wind, he must not keep a glacial distance from his players. More importantly, he must be able to manipulate the team mood, rather than be manipulated by it. The last thing you want is to alienate people.

Tactics

When all's said and done, a captain's primary task is to organise the bowling and set the field. In this sense, tactics and motivation are inextricably linked. It's no good setting a really attacking field knowing the bowlers prefer to be more defensive. This is a sure way to lose runs. Bowlers should have the major say in their field setting. If they don't get it, they'll get very shirty. But, no matter, the captain reserves the right to overrule them. He has the final say.

Field-setting strategies

A lot of field settings will be pre-planned. The team will know that so-and-so tends to hit the ball in a particular area and therefore have men placed to cover it. Alternatively, they may know of a batsman's strength (the hook shot for instance) but leave the area vacant, daring him to play the shot. Or a man might be positioned for the hook shot as a sort of decoy – the bowler never intends giving him the chance to play it. There's a lot of bluff and double bluff in field strategies.

One of the most thorny issues is how long to keep the field 'up' (lots of close catchers). Obviously if the ball is constantly being edged, it's sensible to persist with a predatory slip cordon. But the time will come when edges have ceased or developed a tendency to scoot along the ground towards the boundary (perhaps as the ball gets softer). A high proportion of Test-match runs are acquired through, or wide of, the slips. At some stage, protection (in the form of a third-man fielder) will be needed, which means removing one of the slips. But how soon? That is the perennial question.

It's important to be flexible. Pre-planning is good, but persisting with a ploy if it doesn't work is not. If the captain has put a team in on an apparently damp pitch and they've raced to 90-0 it's time to ditch the attacking fields and opt for Plan B. A stubborn captain is far more likely to rile his team than an adaptable one. The best captains are like the best sailors – they have a feel, maybe an extrasensory perception, of when the wind's changing, and they can alter course accordingly.

Bowling changes

As for bowling changes, although there will be a strategy beforehand, these are very much at the captain's whim. Managing the attack, so that the best bowlers are not over bowled and remain fresh for those vital moments, is a skill that requires acumen, a cool head and some luck. Opening bowlers will normally be rested after a six- or seven-over spell, though they may go on longer if they're taking wickets. Rotating the bowling so that, for instance, all the quicker men get a burst downwind, keeps everyone happy, except the spinner who is lumbered with wheeling away endlessly into a gale.

Sometimes it'll be evident when a bowler is tiring, sometimes it won't. The trick is to relieve him before he sends down that weary over, costing 12 runs. Through a long, tiring day, it's sensible to share the workload.

For instance, it was noticeable how often against the West Indies Nasser Hussain gave his spearhead, Darren Gough, a brief early spell, then brought him back immediately Brian Lara walked to the wicket. As Gough claimed Lara five times for single figures in the series, it's a ploy that can be said to have definitely worked.

Keeping up the pressure

What should always be uppermost in the captain's mind is how to keep the batsmen under pressure – putting bowlers on or fielders in positions that the batters specifically don't like. A batsman who is uncomfortable or frustrated will inevitably get out. There are a-thousand-and-one tactical ruses to prosper in the field: from the obvious (maintain relentless accuracy, as Australia do) to the bizarre (Mike Brearley's overs of slow, head-high lobs with everyone back on the boundary, confused even the most confident batsman).

It's easy to distinguish a good captain from a bad one in the field. The better ones seem always one step ahead of the game, putting bowlers on who immediately take wickets, placing fielders in positions where they stop runs. They have vision and direction. The also-rans 'follow the ball', plugging gaps that have already gushed runs and leaving bowlers on for long spells, letting the game atrophy. A good captain, a man with an agile tactical mind and a perceptive eye, is worth his place in the team for this alone.

England Test Captains and their Records (Post 1977)

	Tests	Won	Lost	Drawn	% won
J M Brearley	31	18	4	9	58.06
I T Botham	12	0	4	8	0
K W R Fletcher	7	1	1	5	14.28
R G D Willis	18	7	5	6	38.88
D I Gower	32	5	18	9	15.62
M W Gatting	23	2	5	16	8.69
G A Gooch	34	10	12	12	29.41
A J Stewart	13	3	7	3	23.07
M A Atherton	52	13	19	20	25.00
N Hussain	16	6	5	5	37.50

Declarations and the Follow-on

Little is written these days about the art of declaring, largely because it isn't very often necessary. Bowlers are so good and pitches so indifferent, teams get rolled over before the captain can even contemplate declaring the innings closed. On the rare occasion that it is an option, however, the timing can make all the difference. If the decision to declare is sometimes an unenviable one, a more pleasant task for the captain is to enforce the follow-on. This happens when team B are all out for 200-or-more runs less than team A's first-innings' total – they can be asked to bat again immediately.

Declarations

Unless one side is so totally in command that the other has no hope of winning, declaring is a sort of balancing act. There should be enough time to bowl the other team out (on average about a day) but not too much more, because this could give the team batting last a greater chance of winning themselves. At the same time there should be a carrot for them too. A team set 300 to win in four hours will just shut up shop and be hard to dismiss. A more tempting 250 in five hours might just lure them into some injudicious shots. Often you have to risk losing to win. (There have, incidentally, been only a handful of occasions when teams have made over 300 to win a Test match in the fourth innings.)

Because of what's at stake, however, most Test captains are pretty cautious when it comes to declarations. Lack of daring declarations on predominantly flat, easy batting pitches on the sub-continent, has guaranteed that the majority of Tests between India and Pakistan (33 out of 47) have been draws.

The follow-on

A captain does not have to enforce the follow-on but being asked to follow on is psychologically damaging, and virtually consigns you to having your backs to the wall for the rest of the match. Usually, batting out the rest of the match to salvage a draw is the best you can hope for. This is why events at Headingley in 1981 were so remarkable. Australia made 401, dismissed England for 174 and enforced the follow-on, as you would. Second time around, England were teetering on 135-7, staring an innings defeat in the face. This was when Ian Botham took the game by the scruff of the neck with a barnstorming century. England eventually totalled 356, leaving Australia 130 to win. Inspirational bowling by Bob Willis gave England an extraordinary 18-run win.

Perhaps as a legacy of this, Test captains are now a little more wary of enforcing the follow-on, especially if their bowlers are tired and not relishing the prospect of more labours in the field. But it's still normally the best option.

Media

These days a captain's work is never done until the last television camera has been switched off and the last scribe has vacated the press box. Media interviews at the beginning and end of the match (and often during it) have become a prerequisite of the captain's job. Many find it a burden and try to avoid them if they can (David Gower actually went to the theatre instead of turning up for one of his own press conferences) or they become monosyllabic. Because of the extensive and varied coverage of Test cricket in the twenty-first century, it's not the easiest of the captain's tasks.

Playing the game

The captain who is up-front and friendly with the media generally gets a good press even if the team is doing badly. But, like England football managers, some have got themselves into trouble with an apparently innocuous comment that gets distorted into something else. It is this that sometimes pushes already severely drained Test captains over the edge.

Test-match captaincy is one of the hardest jobs in sport – the captain is pit-face worker, shift supervisor and trades-union spokesman all rolled into one. They have a lot on their plate, and it's no wonder their own game sometimes suffers. Nasser Hussain's batting average plummeted during 2000, and it wasn't until his last Test innings of the year that he managed to make more than 20.

The Australian Mark Taylor had similar experiences, and there were frequent calls for his head during the early part of their 1997 England tour. Even the English press joined in before the first Test. Taylor's form had become so wretched even taking guard was torturous, and a man from the *Daily Mirror* tried to present him with a special three-foot wide 'Duck bat', when the Australians arrived to play Gloucestershire.

Taylor arrived in the Bristol press box to face the knife-brandishing media. 'You ignored the present from the *Mirror*, does this suggest you've lost your sense of humour?' stabbed one journalist. 'No, I can still laugh at myself, but I don't think I have to stand next to a three-foot bat to prove I'm a humourous chap,' Taylor replied, chuckling. He had the last laugh; he made a century at Edgbaston and six weeks later Australia had won the Ashes, again.

Star players are a captain's best friends. Players like Botham, Warne and Lara can camouflage a multitude of inadequacies and get 'luck' on your side. Without them captaincy is a severe test of character. Taylor has been the outstanding Test captain of the last decade. He was constantly able to rub the lamp and conjure up something. But it helps to have a few genies at your disposal.

UMPIRING

For the last 250 years, at least, two umpires have kept an eye on proceedings on the field. One will stand at the bowler's end to adjudicate no-balls, wides, lbws and fine snicks to the keeper, among other things. The other will loiter at square leg to judge stumpings, run outs and anything else that requires a side-on view. Both will count the number of balls bowled each over. But things are changing for umpires and there is pressure to use more technology in decision making, so the future of umpiring is rather uncertain.

Keepers of the Law

Before the first laws of cricket were drawn up in 1744, the umpires brandished a small stick that had to be touched by the batsman to signal the completion of a run. It was symbolic of their authority, and they remain the sole judges of fair and unfair play – taking action against bowlers who persistently run on to the playing surface, for instance. The fitness of the pitch, light, weather, and the ball itself are also subject to the umpire's approval. A vital phrase throughout the laws of the game is 'if in the opinion of the umpire, etc, etc ...'. No other opinion counts like his.

However, with the advance of technology, the television camera has inevitably been used to help umpires with their decisions, and slow-motion images replayed reveal what happened in those flashing moments. The third umpire, sitting in a small cubicle above the ground, is being increasingly requested to make judgements after consulting the TV monitor. A third umpire is now compulsory at Test matches and there will usually be a fourth too, in reserve, as well as a match referee.

Almost all English professional umpires were first-class players, and several, including David Shepherd and Peter Willey are on the international umpires panel. This provides all umpires for Test matches, one from the home side and one neutral.

Harold 'Dickie' Bird is the most famous of the men in white coats, partly because he was so eccentric, but mainly because he stood in 66 Test matches, more than any other umpire in history.

OUT
The sight all batsmen dread. A batsman can be out in a number of ways but it is the lbw decisions that involve the most agonising wait for the umpire's finger to go up.

Umpiring Signals

Umpires use a unique brand of semaphore to communicate decisions and incidents to players and scorers. Here are the main ones:

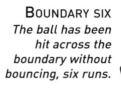

BOUNDARY SIX
The ball has been hit across the boundary without bouncing, six runs.

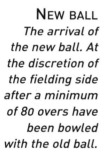

NEW BALL
The arrival of the new ball. At the discretion of the fielding side after a minimum of 80 overs have been bowled with the old ball.

BYE
Run(s) scored by a ball that misses the batsman, wicket and keeper and allows the batsmen to take run(s). Run(s) will be added to the batting total but not to an individual batsman's score.

LAST HOUR
Umpires are the time-keepers, the last hour is significant because there must be at least 20 overs bowled in the final hour.

SHORT-RUN
A run that is disallowed because the batsman has not made his ground.

No-ball
A ball that is disallowed for a variety of reasons (over-stepping the crease being the most common). It counts as one run to the batting side and the bowler has to bowl another ball.

Out
The dreaded signal. There is no argument, the batsman has to go.

Boundary four
A ball crossing the boundary after having bounced gains four runs.

Wide ball
A ball that is too high or too far away from the batsman for him to play a stroke. It counts as one run to the batting side and another ball has to be bowled.

Dead ball
The ball is considered 'dead' (not in play) in various instances, including when it is is in the keeper's hands, when a batsman is out, and when the ball lodges in the batsman's clothing.

Leg bye
Run(s) taken after the ball has struck the batsman's body or leg. He must have been attempting to hit the ball. The leg bye counts as an 'extra'.

JARGONBUSTING
The A–Z of cricket vernacular

A

ACROSS THE LINE – a shot with horizontal bat at right angles to the path of the delivery.

AGRICULTURAL – a hefty shot to the leg-side, sometimes called a 'cow stroke'.

ANALYSIS – a bowler's statistics after a completed innings (or a day's play): e.g. 12-2-36-2, relating to overs bowled, maidens, runs conceded, and wickets taken, always in that order.

ARM BALL – a delivery from a spinner that doesn't turn but goes straight on. You'll often hear a commentator say 'that one went on with the arm'. See p. 103.

AVERAGE – for a batsman this is the total number of runs scored divided by the total number of times he's been out (obviously excluding not outs). E.g. a batsman who has made 300 runs in 12 innings with 2 not outs, has an average of 30. Over 40 is considered a good Test-batting average.
For a bowler it is the number of runs conceded divided by wickets taken. So a bowler who has conceded 1000 runs and taken 40 wickets has an average of 25. Only the best achieve that.

AWAY-SWING – a ball curving in the air away from the right-hand batsman, towards the slips, with the shiny side to the right. (Also known as OUTSWING.) See p. 80.

B

BACK FOOT – the right foot of the right-hand batsman. To a short ball, a batsman may take a step backwards towards the stumps to play the ball off the back foot. See pp. 32, 47.

BACKLIFT – a batsman's first raising of the bat behind himself in readiness for playing a shot. Brian Lara's backlift is a lot more pronounced than most. See pp. 24–25.

BACKING-UP – the non-striking batsman beginning to move up the pitch as the bowler releases, in case there's a chance of a run. See p. 51. Also used to describe fielders getting in place behind the wicket as cover, in case a throw from the outfield is wild.

BAKERLOO – a slang reference to a batsman playing down the wrong line.

BALL DOCTORING/TAMPERING – a number of illegal practices by the fielding side (scratching, applying Vaseline, etc.) to change the ball's condition. See p. 92.

BANG IN – when a fast ball is directed into the middle of the pitch and is intended to rise up at the batsman. The West Indians call this 'putting it in the mud'.

BAT-PAD – a close fielding position on the leg-side (also known as SHORT LEG) to catch the ball ricocheting off the edge of the bat onto the pad (or pad onto bat). See p. 123.

BEAMER – a delivery flying at the batsman's head without bouncing. It's usually accidental and causes the batsman severe heart palpitations if it's straight. It would be unwise to attempt a shot.

BELTER – a flat pitch, very much favouring the batsmen.

BLOB – a batsman scoring nought.

BLOCKHOLE – a place on the crease where the batsman marks his guard. A delivery 'in the blockhole' is one aimed to slide under the bat. See YORKER.

BOUNCER – a fast ball directed into the middle of the pitch intended to leap up around the batsman's head. It used to be called a 'bumper'. At present, only two are allowed per over in Test cricket. See p. 84.

BOUNDARY – the edge of the playing area, delineated by a white line, a rope or a fence. It must be at least 60 yards from the bat in Test matches. There was no such thing in cricket until the 1860s (before that, every hit had to be run). Now, if the ball runs over the boundary it counts as four, irrespective of how many runs the batsmen have completed. A hit that clears the boundary without bouncing is worth six. (Apologies to the initiated, but a man was overheard in a hospitality box at a Lord's Test saying, 'Do they still have sixes in cricket?')

BOX – not the hospitality version, this is an oval shaped protector worn by batsmen, keepers, short legs and, on bumpy outfields, anyone else who values his manhood.

BOWLING CREASE – the front line the bowler must not overstep when delivering the ball. See p. 16.

BUMP BALL – an apparent catch that is not out because the ball has, in fact, been hit hard into the ground.

BUNSEN – rhyming slang for a TURNING WICKET, after bunsen burner.

BYE – a run scored from a ball that passes by the batsman and wicket and is fumbled or missed by the keeper, enabling the batsmen to take a run. The run is added to the batting total but not to the individual batsman's score. See LEG BYE.

C

CAFETERIA BOWLING – lots of loose deliveries that invite a batsman to, literally, 'help himself'.

CARRY YOUR BAT – when an opening batsman is not out when his team are bowled out.

CHARGE – a batsman running down the pitch at the bowler as, or before, he releases the ball. See p. 55.

CHINAMAN – an unconventional ball bowled by a left-arm spinner that

turns in to the right-hand batsman. See p. 109.

CHINESE CUT – a ball grazing the inside edge of the bat and shooting just past the leg stump.

CHIN MUSIC – intimidatory short-pitched bowling aimed at the batsman's head. It was a West Indian expression originally.

CLOSING THE FACE – turning the blade of the bat inwards to hit a ball on the leg-side. See p. 49.

CORDON – the ring of close fielders behind the wicket.

CORRIDOR OF UNCERTAINTY – an area just outside the batsman's off stump. The batsman is unsure whether to play or leave a ball landing here. See p. 83.

COVER/COVER POINT – an off-side fielding position on the line of the batting crease about 25 yards from the bat. Derived from a much closer position that was literally on the point of the bat. A cover drive is a shot towards (and hopefully past) cover point. See p. 124.

CREASE – the areas around the wickets marked with white lines that indicate the extent of the batsman's safe territory (see POPPING CREASE). Also, the area within which the bowler's feet must land when bowling a ball (bowling crease and return crease). See p. 16.

CROSS BAT – bat swung in a horizontal motion, across the line of the ball.

CUT – an off-side shot played with a downward, axe-like movement of the bat. It is also used to describe the movement of the ball off the pitch, as in 'cut back'.

CUTTER – a fastish delivery that deviates after pitching, usually because the bowler has flicked his wrist slightly across the ball in release. Also, a batsman who favours the cut shot.

D

DANGER AREA – the business area of the pitch in line with the stumps, which must not be damaged by bowlers following through after they have bowled, or batsmen taking a run.

DEAD BALL – the umpire will call this if the ball has become lodged in the batsman's pad or clothing, or if it has slipped out of the bowler's hand and dribbled into the outfield. The ball is always 'dead' once it is safely in the

keeper's gloves and no one is attempting a run.

DECLARATION – a captain can declare his team's innings closed at any time (i.e. before all the wickets have fallen). This is particularly likely if a team have built up a big score and fancy a few overs bowling in the evening, or when setting up a run chase on the last day. See p. 142.

DOLLY – an easy catch that lobs to the fielder without him having to move. Its derivation is thought to be from the Anglo-Indian word 'dolly' meaning a friendly offering of food.

DOT BALL – a delivery off which no runs are scored, so called because it is recorded in the scorebook as a plain dot.

DRAW – this is not quite in the football sense of the term, since it is a more inconclusive result in cricket. Basically, any match in which the side batting last falls short of the required target but isn't bowled out (or any match ruined by bad weather).

DRIFTER – a spin bowler's delivery that doesn't turn but deviates gently in the air.

DUCK – a score of nought, originating from 'making a duck's egg'.

E F

ECONOMY RATE – a statistic in a bowler's analysis that indicates how many runs he has conceded per over.

EXTRAS – runs that aren't scored off the bat. These constitute wides, no-balls, byes and leg byes.

FACE – the front of the bat, so the bit that you're supposed to hit the ball with.

FARMING THE STRIKE – a batsman who doesn't let his less able partner face much of the bowling, usually by pinching a single at the end of each over, is said to be farming the strike.

FIELDING POSITIONS – see the diagram on p.129.

FINE – a ball that deflects off the bat without changing its course much.

FINGER SPIN – spin applied more by tweaking the fingers than by flexing the wrist. A conventional off spinner is regarded as a finger spinner, though this is misleading because he uses his wrist to turn the ball as well.

FIRST CLASS – matches of at least three-days duration played by a recognised county, state, zonal or representative sides in any of the Test-playing countries.

FLASH – an uninhibited (often wild) stroke at a fairly wide delivery.

FLIER – can mean a very fast dangerous pitch or rapid run scoring at the beginning of an innings – 'West Indies have got off to a flier'.

FLIPPER – a back spinner 'flipped' or squeezed out of the front of the hand by a leg-break bowler. It skids low after pitching, is difficult to play and even more difficult to master. See p. 112.

FOLLOW-ON – this is when the batting team is asked to go in again because their first innings finished 200 or more runs behind the opposition's total. (In county cricket the differential is 150.) Usually it shuts the team following-on out of the game and the best they can hope for is a draw. Botham's heroics at Headingley in 1981 created the only time in the twentieth century when a side won a Test having been asked to follow on.

FOOTHOLDS – the area within the crease lines where the bowler lands to deliver the ball. They can get quite deep and rutted as the match progresses and have to be filled in with special clay.

FOURBALL – a wide or overpitched delivery that is asking to be hit to the boundary.

FRONT FOOT – the batsman's foot closest to the bowler when he's standing sideways at the wicket (the left foot in the case of a right-hand batsman). A shot 'off the front foot' is one played with the weight on that front leg.

FULL TOSS – a ball which doesn't bounce before reaching the batsman. Normally an accident, and, unless it's very high or swinging viciously, an easy ball to score off. See FOURBALL.

G

GARDENING – the repairing of damaged or disturbed bits of the pitch by a batsman using his bat. Often this is a bit of self-reassurance by the batsman after a good delivery, patting down some non-existent gremlin in the surface.

GATE – the gap left between bat and pad by the batsman that the ball could go (or has gone) through. See p. 81.

GLANCE – a delicate shot, usually to leg, that has deflected rather than assaulted the ball.

GOLDEN DUCK – a batsman getting out for nought first ball.

GOOD-LENGTH BALL – a ball landing in a spot where, especially if it's straight, the batsman can't easily attack it. It may also make him uncertain whether to play back or forward to it. The place varies for different bowlers. For quick men it will pitch 4-6 yards in front of the batsman, for spinners it will be 3-4 yards in front, or '10 paces' as Ray Illingworth always said. See p. 48.

GOOGLY – a leg break that is bowled out of the back of the hand that makes the ball spin in the opposite direction (i.e. from left to right). It's a hard ball to detect from 22 yards away, and is so called because, when it was first discovered in the 1890s, it made the batsman 'goggle' with surprise. See p. 110–111.

GREEN TOP – a pitch that has a lot of visible live grass, greeted with feverish anticipation by fast bowlers.

GRUBBER – a ball which shoots low along the ground after pitching. The Australian version is a mullygrubber.

GUARD – a batsman's preferred standing place at the wicket. He 'takes guard' by holding his bat up vertically in front of the stumps and asking the umpire which stump it is covering. He then marks the place with the edge of the bat. See p. 21 and BLOCKHOLE.

GULLY – a close fielding position alongside the slip cordon, so called because it is in the gap or 'gully' between slip and cover point.

H

HALF-VOLLEY – a ball pitching close to the batsman that he can drive easily without risk of hitting the ball in the air.

HEAVY BALL – a delivery from a medium-paced bowler that is quicker than it looks, the ball hits the bat harder or higher than you'd expect.

HELD UP – a ball angling into the batsman, which moves slightly away off the pitch (see LEG-CUTTER). It's Courtney Walsh's natural delivery.

HOLE OUT – an attempted big hit that doesn't come off but ends up easily caught in the outfield.

HOOK – a cross-batted shot to a ball rising above chest height, usually played by swivelling inside the line and helping the ball on its way. See pp. 40–41.

I J K

INNINGS – used to describe a team's turn at batting and an individual batsman's time batting. Winning 'by an innings' means one team has scored more in their only batting turn than the other has in two complete efforts.

INSWING – a ball curving in the air from left to right (to a right-handed batsman). The greatest modern exponent was Imran Khan.

IN THE V – shots played in a narrow V shaped area either side of the bowler, with the batsman being the base of the V. In other words, straight beating.

JAFFA – a widely used term meaning an unplayable ball – one that deviates or spins alarmingly off the pitch. The origin could be related to the delivery being 'juicy'.

JAG – a ball deviating sharply off the pitch.

KING PAIR – a batsman out twice first ball for nought in the same match.

L

LAP – another word for the sweep stroke.

See p. 56–57.

LEADING EDGE – a ball that loops off the outside or front edge because the bat face has been turned inwards too early.

LBW – one of the most common ways of being out. The ball hits the batsman on the pad in line with the stumps. However, the ball has to satisfy a number of criteria before a batsman can be given out leg before wicket. See pp. 18–19.

LEG-BREAK/SPIN – a ball turning from leg to off (right to left) to right-handed batsman. It was a fading art until the emergence of Shane Warne rejuvenated it. See pp. 110–111.

LEG-BYE – a run scored off a ball that is deflected off the batsman by something other than the bat or the hand holding the bat.

LEG-CUTTER – a straightish ball to a right-hander that suddenly deviates or jags away towards the slips off the pitch. This can happen by accident – caused by the ball landing on the seam – or be deliberately extracted by the bowler tweaking his wrist sideways as he releases. See pp. 78–79.

LEG-SIDE – the area of the field behind a batsman's legs standing in his normal position at the crease.

LENGTH – the place where the ball lands. Used in conjunction with the words 'good', 'poor', 'full', 'short' and 'back-of-a'. See pp. 48–49.

LINE – the direction the ball is travelling in, i.e. off stump line is a ball aimed at off stump.

LONG HOP – a very short ball, usually an accident, that sits up and begs to be dispatched to the boundary.

LOOP – a slow bowler who imparts a lot of spin on the ball, making it dip deceptively late in flight, is described as 'having a good loop'.

M

MAIDEN – an over in which no runs were scored. Derives from the idea of unproductivity. If there are byes in an over, but no runs scored off the bat, it still counts as a maiden.

MAKER'S NAME – a straight shot played with the manufacturer's logo (on the face of the bat) visible throughout.

MANHATTAN – a bar graph relaying runs scored per over. A period of heavy scoring will resemble the New York skyline.

N

NELSON – the dreaded score of 111. When this total is reached, the superstitious custom is for the batting team off the pitch (and umpire David Shepherd) to take their feet off the ground. The name was coined in the mistaken belief that Nelson had one eye, one arm and one leg: in fact, he had two legs.

NEW BALL – a brand new ball will be issued to the fielding side at the beginning of an innings. In Tests, the fielding side are entitled to another new ball after 80 overs with the old one.

NICK – a ball grazing the edge of a bat (shortening of 'snick').

NIGHTWATCHMAN – a tail-end batsman sent in near the end of the day above his usual position to protect more recognised batsmen from having to face the last few overs. See p. 66.

NIP/NIP BACKER – bowlers who have 'nip' seem to make the ball gather pace off the pitch. A 'nip backer' is a ball that suddenly darts into the batsman from outside off stump.

NO-BALL – the umpire will call a no-ball when: 1. The bowler has completely overstepped the front line of the crease. 2. He has cut the side line with his back foot. 3. The bowler has 'thrown' the delivery (i.e. his arm has extended from bent to straight on release). 4. There are more than two fielders behind square on the legside. A no-ball counts one to the total (two in county cricket) and must be re-bowled. In theory, the batsman is getting a free hit since he can't be out bowled, caught, lbw or stumped off a no-ball (though he can be run out). In practice, however, the umpire's no-ball call is invariably too late for the batsman to take advantage of it.

NURDLE – to score runs by nudging the ball into gaps.

O

OFF-BREAK/SPIN – a ball turning into the right hander- from off to leg (from left to right). See pp. 102–103.

OFF-CUTTER – a much faster off-break, bowled by a quicker bowler that cuts into the batsman, either fortuitously because it pitched on the seam, or by design, the bowler having cut his fingers across the ball on release.

OFF THE MARK – a batsman who gets 'off the mark' has scored his first run.

OFF-SIDE – the side of the ground facing the batsman in his normal stance (opposite of leg-side).

ON-SIDE – same as leg-side (the opposite of off-side).

ON THE UP – a front-foot drive played to a ball that is not a half volley, hit higher on the bounce, i.e. as the ball is 'on its way up'. See p. 45.

OUT – there are eleven possible ways of being out, but only five common ones – bowled, caught, lbw, stumped and run out. See p. 17.

OUTSWING – a ball curving out from the stumps towards the slips. See AWAY SWING

OVER – each over is made up of six legitimately bowled balls (from the same end). Four balls once constituted an over, and in Australia it was eight until the late 1970s, which in that heat was a stern test of a fast bowler's stamina.

OVERPITCH – a ball of very full length that is easy to score off. Bowlers who consistently overpitch won't be kept on long.

OVER THE WICKET – a right-arm bowler delivering from the standard position with the umpire on his right.

P

PADDLE – a gentle sweep shot, dabbed rather than hit, as if using an oar.

PAIR – a batsman making two noughts in a match (it looks like a pair of spectacles). Graham Gooch made a pair in his first Test, but finished up as England's all-time top run scorer.

PITCH – it's 22 yards long and 10 feet wide and has been ever since 1744. The length was consistent with a 'chain' (a unit of land measurement in the seventeenth century). Pitch also means the bounce of the ball.

PLAY ON – deflecting the ball into the stumps with the edge of the bat.

PLUMB – a very flat pitch, or an indisputable lbw decision.

POINT – similar fielding position to cover point, about 20 yards from the bat . It was once right on the 'point' of the bat, equivalent to the modern 'silly-point' position.

POPPING CREASE – the line marking the limit of the batsman's ground (4 feet in front of the stumps). Its name has lingered since the days when there was a small hole on this line which the batsman had to jab the bat into when completing a run, before the bowler or fielder 'popped' the ball in it. A practice that resulted in quite a few damaged fingers.

PUDDING – a very slow, spongy pitch.

PULL – a back-foot leg-side shot, distinct from the hook because the pull is played to a ball that hasn't risen as high. See pp. 40–41.

R

RABBIT – tail-ender with little batting ability who is not expected to last long.

RETIRE – if a batsman retires hurt, he can resume his innings whenever he's fit to do so after the fall of a wicket. Occasionally, a batsman will be 'retired out' to give other batsman a chance – this happens in matches against lesser opposition (e.g. county matches against Oxford or Cambridge, or England tour matches against 'a President's XI'). In this case it is counted as a dismissal.

RETURN CREASE – the lines at right angles to the batting (popping) crease, stretching back behind the wicket, which the bowler must not cross with his back foot when delivering the ball.

REVERSE SWEEP – a relatively modern shot that is played by inverting the wrists and turning the blade so the back of the bat faces the bowler, then, going down on one knee to sweep the ball on the off-side rather than the leg-side. See pp. 58–59.

REVERSE SWING – another recently discovered phenomenon that causes the ball in certain dry conditions, to swing in the opposite direction to conventional swing. It generally curves more, and later in flight, than normal swing. Because of the dry, cracked nature of their pitches, and their proliferation of fast bowlers, the Pakistanis were world leaders in this art, but other countries have now caught up. See p. 91.

RIP – slang for spin. To 'give it a real rip', is to try to turn the ball sideways.

ROUGH – scuffed area of the pitch wide of the stumps created by bowlers following through. Spinners will often aim at it later in the match.

ROUND THE WICKET – a delivery from the unconventional side of the umpire that is used to try to make something happen or to left-hand batsmen so the bowler has a better view of the stumps. See p. 94.

RUNNER – a dismissed batsman who is summoned to run between the wickets for an injured colleague. He must wear exactly the same protective gear (i.e. pads, helmet, etc) as the injured player.

S

SANDSHOE CRUSHER – an Australian term for a ball pitching on the batsman's toes. See YORKER.

SEAM – the ridge of stitching that holds the two halves of the ball together. To 'seam' the ball means to make it deviate or change direction by landing it on the seam. A 'seamer' is a bowler who relies mainly on movement off the pitch (e.g. Angus Fraser or Glenn McGrath) rather than through the air.

SHORT LEG – a very close fielding position on the leg-side, almost in the batsman's hip pocket.

SLEDGING – verbal abuse of the batsman, attempting to break down his resistance as if with a sledgehammer. Some sledges are humorous and some plain abusive. Typical examples would be 'D'you want a bell in it mate?' or 'I'll bowl you a piano, see if you can play that', from a bowler to a batsman who keeps missing the ball. Originating in

Australia, sledging is not a recent habit. Back in 1933, Harold Larwood said 'A cricket tour in Australia would be a most delightful period in one's life if one were deaf.'

SLIP – a fielder close to the wicket-keeper, hoping to catch a 'slip' (i.e. an edge) by the batsman. Using two or three slips is common, more is rare.

SLOG – a hefty, cross-batted shot to leg, like a 'cow shot'.

SLOWER BALL – it has become very much in vogue for fast bowlers to develop a delivery which, with little apparent change of action, arrives much slower and makes the batsman play too early. There are various forms. See pp. 96–97.

SQUARE – the area at right angles to the pitch on either side. Also used for the collection of pitches in the middle of the playing field.

STANDING BACK/STANDING UP – the two wicket-keeper's positions: the former used for fast bowlers, the latter, right up to the stumps for spinners. See pp. 132–134.

STOCK BALL – a bowler's normal ball, the one they bowl most regularly.

STRIKE RATE – for a batsman, this indicates how many runs

they score per 100 balls received (10 runs off 20 balls equals a strike rate of 50). For a bowler, the figure tells you how many balls they bowled per wicket taken (so a strike rate of 48 means a bowler takes a wicket every 8 overs).

SWEEP — a shot played to leg, usually down on one knee so the edge of the bat brushes the ground. See pp. 56–57.

SWING — the curve of the ball in the air (see AWAY-SWING and INSWING). Well known current swing bowlers include Wasim Akram and Darren Gough.

T

THIRD MAN — a fielder on the boundary behind the slips. Originally it was closer to the bat to augment the regular positions of slip and point so was called 'third man up'.

TON — a century (100 runs by a single batsman on one innings).

TRACK — common vernacular for the pitch.

TURNING WICKET — a pitch receptive to spin, which is usually very dry and cracked.

TWELFTH MAN — the player who wasn't selected in the final eleven but who can act as substitute fielder if another is incapacitated. Often the official

12th man is allowed home (or to play for his county) and a spritely youngster is brought in to run errands and do the substitute fielding. He is not allowed to bat or bowl.

U W

UNCOVERED PITCHES — pitches used to be left open to the elements if play was suspended for rain, which, it is often argued, created a rich diversity of conditions (the sticky dog – a drying wicket – for instance). It is certainly true that English pitches are much more uniform now that they are completely covered at the first sign of a black cloud.

WAGON WHEEL — a batsman's scorechart, each spaghetti line superimposed on the outfield signifying the direction (and value) of a scoring shot. These reveal a batsman's strengths and favourite scoring avenues.

WALK — a batsman heading for the pavilion, without waiting for an umpire to give him out (usually after finely edging the ball). You're more likely to find a four-leaf clover than see a batsman walk in a Test match these days.

WICKET — not only a dismissal, and the collective word for the stumps, but often it also means the pitch, a use of 'wicket' purists don't like.

WORK — to manoeuvre a straight ball through the legside by turning the blade inwards using a deft wrist action.

WRIST SPIN — spin that is mainly imparted by flexing the wrist rather than the fingers. Leg-spin falls into this bracket, although some off-spinners, notably the big-spinning Sri Lankan Muttiah Muralitharan, do too.

WRONG 'UN — another term for the googly, or any other ball that spins in an unexpected direction.

Y Z

YORKER — fast ball pitching close to, or level with, the batsman's feet, aimed to go under the bat. It derives from an old phrase 'to york' or 'put yorkshire on' someone, which was common parlance for hoodwinking or deceiving them. See pp. 84–85.

ZOOTER — one of a leg spinner's subtler variations, this ball is slipped out of the hand without much spin imparted and tends to dip into the batsman. The term was coined by Shane Warne and his spin 'doctor' Terry Jenner, perhaps partly to enhance his mystique.

Index

Acknowledgments

The author would like to thank David Brook at Channel 4 for all his energy and ideas and Jeff Foulser and Gary Franses at Sunset and Vine for their constant enthusiasm, innovation and imagination. Thanks also to Alan Ryan for his painstaking research. Thanks to Sunset and Vine, the BBC and TWI for making their pictures available, to the Association of Umpires and Scorers and Tom Smith for allowing their drawings to be reprinted, and to Damien and Claire and all at Studio Cactus for the design. Special thanks to Mark Nicholas and Richie Benaud for finding the time to supply their contributions.

A million thanks to Gwen McCann for her dedication and thought in putting it all together, and to my wife Tanya for her encouragement and endurance of long, monosyllabic evenings.